EBRAHIM ESSA

EB KOYBIE

A memoir of shenanigans
between Durban and Bombay

SOCIAL BANDIT MEDIA

Eb Koybie: A memoir of shenanigans between Durban and Bombay

Copyright @ Ebrahim Essa and Azad Essa; All rights reserved

ISBN: 978-0-620-85921-9

First Published in South Africa by Social Bandit Media in 2019

Cover photograph: Pahalgam, Indian occupied Kashmir, 1967

Edited by Azad Essa

Cover design, copy editing & typesetting: Samina Anwary

EB KOYBIE

A memoir of shenanigans
between Durban and Bombay

To those who were denied a childhood

CONTENTS

Foreword

For as long as I can remember, my father has been a
storyteller.

Be it about his childhood growing up in Mayville
surrounded by a mythical thicket and a waterfall, or
about Don Diego aka Zorro's hideout at the bottom
of Palmiet valley cleaning up the neighbourhood of
crime at night, my childhood was an endless stream
of make believe that made me feel as if I lived within
a parable itself.

Growing up, my sister Shenaaz and I would
listen as Dad would send us on one guilt trip after
another for wanting a Sony walkman, when he
"grew up without electricity", or for wanting a new
pair of Reeboks when he had "to walk to school
without any shoes". I was reminded repeatedly that
if he, as a 7-year-old, could do his business while
fighting banshees in the only toilet outside the
house in the middle of the night, the least I could
do as a 10-year-old, was to make an effort not to
piss all over the rubbish bin when I ambled over to
the toilet next to the bedroom in the middle of the
night.

It would be years until I'd realise that this was the
immigrant way; shame-guilt the kids into making
a future for themselves. Naturally, the stories were
designed to shape our sensibilities, put the world

into context, and put us firmly in our place when we stepped out of line.

But beyond the immigrant way, Dad gifted us the opportunity to imagine; to project, draw linkages between places, think independently, remember our insignificance in the story of time, and to focus on building experiences in shaking up our environment rather than the spurious focus on the accumulation of things. We were never burdened by ritual or fear of the unknown. Where other kids were told to run inside at dusk for fear of djinns, we were told to come home at sunset to avoid being knocked by a wayward bus.

He also imparted a sense of civic participation. If you wanted something done, you'd have to make it happen, or at least die trying. Certainly, the seed of journalism was planted by a mix of my mother's interest in the world and my father's insistence on trying to make sense of it.

I do suspect that his prolific letter writing to newspapers has probably achieved a lot more than my work as a journalist.

And this book is part of that thirst to contribute, to cement, to lay down our speck of history on the infinite canvas of the universe.

Eb Koybie, loosely translated from Memon as *'And for that matter, anybody'*, is a phrase coined by my Dad, which became somewhat of an inside joke between him and his father (see page 170). Though it was pure mischief on his part, it is an example of a tremendous talent with words. I see it another way, too. *Eb Koybie* is not merely a memoir of one person, but the chronicling of a unique moment in our family, community, country and world history.

As a child of the late 40s and 50s, he was born early to apartheid and late to India's independence. It would take time before he understood either as a home or a place of safety.

My great grandfather Essa first traveled to South Africa close to 100 years ago, and Dad was born two years before apartheid began. These were precarious times. And like so many of his generation to wax lyrical about growing up during those times despite the hardships, I wanted him to chronicle a time that we have yet to fully understand.

And the story moves, from Mayville to Grey Street and Albert Street, to Andheri and Ghatanji, in many ways because of the restrictions of the time.

His is the story of so many first generation South Africans of Indian origin, who grew up on the romance and escape of Hindi cinema and the gallantry of often-banned comic book heroes. These stories shaped his way of seeing. It is no surprise that his memories are almost interminably linked to those of the Hindi songs from classic Indian films from the 40s and 50s and sometimes later.

So when I finally convinced him to write down his stories, he neatly slotted a film to each memory as if there would be no memory without the background music.

I wanted these stories documented, so that they might give us a peek into the lives of our elders; be it him or anyone else, especially during a time when their sense of place was so fluid.

And yet, the best part of this book is that it is both insightful and funny. It is part satire and part memoir. Like Dad, it never takes itself too seriously, well, and unless, it is compelled to.

The most difficult part of putting this book together was figuring out what to leave out; there are stories upon stories that couldn't fit in; others less fictional than others, but great stories nonetheless. We had many arguments over the way stories were edited. It was only the intervention of my mother that kept this baby afloat.

Still, I understand that he is not going to love all the final edits. Like a classic writer he is precious with his words, even when they don't make sense. And true to character, I wouldn't be surprised if he rejects this copy and hands out his own version held together by a couple of staples.

But this is the painful process of organising thoughts and documenting memories that have long been made.

I have to acknowledge that this book is in part inspired by my father's own writing about his father who passed away in 1974.

This year marks 40 years since he completed the first edition of that short biography of Suliman Essa Patel, which is published as an additional chapter in this book.

We lose our stories and we lose our history; we lose our history and we lose our compass.

Mostly, if we don't remember, we stand to lose out on a good laugh.

Azad Essa
Maplewood, New Jersey, October 2019

Preface

It is 1951. I am five. My brother Walla and sister Halima have just left for school. I am not old enough to join them. Even if I were, there is just no space in government schools. But I still insist on my own pre-packed lunch. I am, at this point, the youngest; therefore by tradition, spoilt.

Mother quickly rigs up some pineapple jam sandwiches, wraps them in thick tissue paper and hands them to me. I throw up a tantrum. I want it to be wrapped further in brown paper. Just like my brother's and sister's. I then rush off very business-like, with a tiny box-like school bag and head for my hideout under the staircase.

This temporary stockroom has acquired permanent status. It has no lights. A broken wheelbarrow, rusted-beyond-repair years ago and carrying a useless collection of drums, half-filled with old, dry paint, limewash, paraffin and paintbrushes, blocks my way to the interior. No problem. I merely scramble over and crawl to the dead end of the storage area, locate a half-broken metal bucket and seat myself comfortably on it. In near complete darkness, I fearlessly fight off cobwebs from my face and ignore the musty mixture of smells from the dampness, urine, rat-excrement and the leftover body odour of Laangvaan. He is the tall, one-eyed, semi-crippled handyman; dismissed more than a year ago for stealing Walla's woollen, sleeveless grey jersey from the clothesline. Allegedly stealing, I should add.

I decide furiously but carefully, that it is already the first break of my busy schedule and time for jam sandwiches.

I unpack the fresh, hand-sliced Baker's brown bread splattered with the complementary dairy, Mooi River butter, and dig my milk-teeth into them. The excess jam oozes out; half makes its way into my mouth, the other half slips down my shirt, shorts and shoes, settling into a dark red gel with the dust on the floor. Of course, I cannot really see any of this. It is dark and quiet.

Suddenly I am jolted by the sound of Mother's crisp voice.

"Acchaa! Yahaan ho. Khane se pehle, haath saaf karo. Varna…"

"Okay Ma. Will you tell me the story after I have my breakfast and have a bath?"

"Phir se?"

And this is how I remember it.

It is 1920 in an insignificant village called Jodiya, near Rajkot in Gujarat, India.

Behind my great grandfather's house – a once-luxurious hut made from mud, and roofed with thatch – two skinny cows stand side by side. Flapping at their behinds, a goat and two chickens heckle at the dust. My uncles, Ahmed, Mohammed, Ismail, and my father and hero, Suliman, squat on the dry hay around the animals and play pat-a-cake with the drying dung.

Dressed in tassels and a matching fez, my great grandfather and namesake, Ebrahim, stands proudly amidst the dung, resisting the urge to play. Beside him, my grandfather Essa – known for a maturity beyond his years – blows plumes of salty smoke into the faces of his sons playing with the soft serve. My grandfather was always a strict believer in injustice for all.

"Now look here," my great grandfather, Ebrahim begins. "It is obvious that we are in for a hard year. This drought is going to kill our chance of swindling the farmers. I say we need to expand our horizons."

"What are you proposing?" grandfather Essa replies. Ebrahim answers:

"I say we head South."

"You mean Madras?"

"No. I mean South Africa. I have heard from reliable sources that the place is overflowing in gold. So, who is in?"

My father, Suliman, known for his bravery, dared to ask "Why?".

Suffice to say, Suliman is called a ghadera and given a thwack for asking, and the meeting is adjourned.

The next afternoon, great-grandfather calls up another meeting. This time it's held purposely in front of the open yard.

He wants to get this over with fast.

"This is the plan. We catch the 6:22am bullock-cart service to Viramgam first thing after fajr namaz tomorrow. Then we jump on Rajkot Express and the Saurastra Broadgauge to Bombay the next day. From there we head out to Ballard Pier, and via Mombasa, we make our way to Durban on BI Lines."

DURBAN HARBOUR

The first friendly greeting they receive at Durban Harbour, as they walk down the gangplank is from a big Afrikaner.

"Where do you think you blerrie coolies are taking those things?"

He is referring to the she-camel, black bull and three goats that Ismail and Mohammed are guiding down the gangplank. Mohammed hated personal slights.

He quickly replied, "See here, Malan! You can't really refer to us as your everyday, normal, Indian-typecast coolies. We are actually not even your run-of-the-mill canecutters. We are Memons."

And true to name, the family began hustling, first with building material, then with demolition equipment. Until Father – Suliman – discovered gold.

Father decided in 1937, that smuggling gold to India was the easiest way to make it big and show up the Baker Brothers crowd. My grandfather, Essa, agreed but ordered that Father's brother-in-law Dawood accompany him. It would keep Father honest, he said.

Father moved with the cache of gold – so cleverly welded in the belly of the Plymouth – past Molver Road out of Mayville, overland to Mombasa and finally shipped it, car and all, to Madras.

The plan was so simple that there was no way it could fail. At Madras, an agent would introduce them to an immediate buyer. There would be no questions asked. They would be paid a set amount with which Suliman would open a bank account in the family name, to which he would have sole withdrawing rights. He would then return to South Africa, pick up more gold dust and hit the road. He would only stop once the Baker Brothers crowd conceded in front of the Jodiya Panchayat that we, the Patels, were greater than them. But as soon as Father and Dawood-bha reached Madras, they were arrested and deported to South Africa, via Shanghai. Embarrassed and gutted that the smuggling hadn't worked out, the family returned to cutting wood and breaking down old buildings for a living. Father, now ostracised for his glorious smuggling failure, joined Mr Andrew in the scrap-metal scrap business. Andy's Scrap Yard, as it was known, was located at the corner of Queen and Albert Streets in the Durban city centre.

Meanwhile, we lived in Mayville around 8km outside of the city.

I

48 WINDSOR ROAD

*I was born on April 9, 1946. I was the fourth child in a line
of two daughters Hawabai and Halima – and a son named
Yusuf, whom we all called Walla.*

*We all lived under one roof in Mayville – a neighbour-
hood south west of the Durban city centre – a predomi-
nantly Indian suburb full of tin, wood and brick houses.
Our home had been built by Father. Grandfather Essa had
provided the materials, and Father designed and supervised
its construction. But we still paid Grandfather Essa rent for
living on this property.*

*The house was located on top of a hill, had a rectangu-
lar shape, a tin roof, and quaint circular windows on each
side of the front door that faced Windsor Road. There was
a short staircase leading to a garden with lemon trees and
pink-purple-white Christmas flowers. There was a long,
straight flight of concrete steps running down the middle of
the hill flanked by a stepped lawn, complete with a bird-
bath and different species of flowers at each level. I recall
some rent-generating outbuildings on the right hand side.*

*At the bottom of the hill, on the left, was an extra toilet-
with-a-bucket system. Nobody knew why it was there.
No one used it, but there was always this horrible smell
around it. At odd times, smoke used to emanate from the
top of this mysterious edifice.*

Mother (c. 1965)

It was haunted, Walla said, also advising that I never go there. Then one-day Grandfather Essa caught Walla smoking his C to Cs or Westminster 85s inside the toilet. It took me years to make the connection.

MA

I was often alone at home with Mother. Father was at work. My siblings at school.

Hawabai, my elder sister, was living with my grandmother in town. Nobody could explain why. I suspect that it had something to do with a "stalker on Main Road" following her to school. Hawabai said the stalker told her friends that he would "kidnap that Snow White".

Instead of complaining about the predator, she spent her time hiding from him. Then she decided to stop attending school to save the family honour, learned how to cook at grandmother's and stayed illiterate forever.

Mother was always old as far as I can remember.

Thin, frail, hunched due to infantile tuberculosis, she was also seen as an enigma. Her wit forever inappropriate, she was always in trouble with the in-laws. I loved being around her.

She had a skill with words. Hindi, Gujarati, Urdu, Tamil, Marathi. She could make words dance, despite being unable to read or write. Mother hummed songs from the Hindi films, and sang morose Gujarati laments.

"Jhole rajah, jarman jeethi ne, vela aawjo"
"O brave Indian soldier, kick the German's arse and return home early"

Father (c. 1957)

I am not sure if she knew what she was singing about.

I have always loved the tunes from the Hindi films of the day.

It was actually Mother who also taught me how to operate the old gramophone left behind by Grandfather Essa when he moved out to the city. This introduction to Indian music became the foundation for my craze over certain tunes and lyrics. Many of the films of the day marked different episodes in my life and whenever I hear them, vivid memories of actual events fill my mind.

DILLAGI

Our house in Mayville was surrounded by a thicket of bushes and trees.

One morning, *Dillagi* floated through the greenery. It wouldn't be the first time music came to visit us.

Rattan – as the legend goes – reverberated throughout the war years here, over the gentle green slopes covered with slinga berry trees.

Zohrabai Ambala's *Rimjhim Barse Badarwa* and *Ankhiyan Milake* whistled between the branches of guava bushes, and bounced off the birdbaths creating a resonance exclusive to the valley of my Mayville. Oh, Mayville. So sad, so glorious.

Nevertheless, one morning I made up my mind to find the source of "Dillagi".

While Mother was battling with the coal-stove, I snuck out through the back gate and headed out to find Suraiya. I hopped over broken tree trunks, roots, and brave monster flies competing for dog shit strewn across the jungle. In a rare clearing of the forest, I found a wood and iron shack with two windows. Black smoke curled its way up from the thin tin chimney.

Suraiya's voice turned out to be much louder and Naushad's music gripped me with its magic. Could it really have been her; the beautiful Goddess Suraiya herself, inside that shack?

The door was unbolted and I hid behind a tree in fear. A short, wrinkled lady stepped out with a cigarette dangling from her mouth, and some garbage in her hand. She emptied the dirt into a metal drum. This was not Suraiya. This was the witch from *Hansel and Gretel*.

My sister Halima, also known as Gigi, hadn't warned me that she lived so close to our house. I turned around and ran home. I could hear her chasing me with a broomstick as I tried to quickly retrace my path out of the thick forest. I stumbled over fresh human shit. I got home, breathless. Mother wanted to know where I had been and why I was stinking.

SHAITAAN

Most Indian basketwomen in Durban seemed to be of South Indian origin. Uneducated and unskilled, they were either wives of very lowly paid workers or of unemployed husbands. Some of them were widows with very young children and no other source of income. Maybe some were millionaires who just liked to sell vegetables in the morning, but this certainly wasn't my impression.

They would catch the first bus in the morning to the Wholesale Indian Market in Warwick Avenue, then either walk to the various flats and houses in and around the City, or catch a bus and sell their fresh produce at a low profit, to people in the sub-urbs.

Carrying heavy baskets for miles, through all types of weather while dressed in saris was no sim-ple task. Besides delivering very fresh produce, they always brought some new stories, some new gossip, to your door.

On this particular day in 1951, I could see Mother attending to Amma-auntie , our usual basketwoman, from the landing outside the verandah. She was sell-ing karela, double beans, dudhi, bhindi and gawar, at the bottom of the short staircase leading to the gar-den.

I was not particularly interested. I had my own VROOMVROOM! motor car in the form of an old discarded 12″ tyre.

As I pushed it around I noticed Mother's tummy. She was hunching over on her haunches, picking the best vegetables from the basket whilst exchanging the juiciest, raunchy quips with the Amma-auntie.

My motor-tyre was now revving at a high speed at the top of the stairs. I was in top gear. My one eye was on my own speedometer, the other on Mother at the bottom. There was something odd about the shape of her stomach.

The tyre slipped out of my fingers and rolled down at high speed. I watched in horror. Before I could scream anything worth shouting in those circum-stances, it hit fragile Mother on the hump of her hunched back.

She plummeted almost head first onto the basket of dhania, double beans, carrots and karela.

She cursed me in her choicest vernacular. And held her stomach. "Are you trying to kill your brother?!"

She was pregnant. With Ahmed, my fourth sibling.

PEHLA KADAM

I should have been in school by 1952 but there was no space available at any government school. My father took me to a preschool in Bristow Road, run by a retired principal and his son.

I think the teacher's name was Mr Safla.

It was a makeshift, informal school. I doubt anyone important recognised it as a place of education.

The venue was an outbuilding with a division to separate the big boys from the even bigger boys. The senior students – whose ages ranged between 10 and 12 – were taught by the father, whilst new arrivals aged 6 to 9, were taught by the son.

Mr Safla senior was a bespectacled, short, stockily-built gentleman.

He always wore a white shirt, a tie and a tweed coat. He didn't smile, except when he was caning the boys.

The wrist speed of this old man was incredible. He moved from Naeem to Imran like a nifty swordsman. It was as if he resented that he held a cane and not a blade. He also taught us some English words and how to count.

"Abbas! Come to the front of the class, do 100 sit-ups and repeat it twice. Else you will be forced to do it 16 times over the next four days."

Safla Junior looked even more serious than this father. He was tall, fair, with a short blackback and sides. He was rather handsome, I thought.

There was one major difference between father and son. Junior refused to smile even whilst caning the boys.

I was the youngest amongst the younger kids. I automatically qualified to sob, holler, wail, kick, and refuse to release Mother's hand as she attempted to abandon me at the entrance of the school every morning. In Mother's presence, son-of-Safla would reassure me ever-so-kindly, and gently show me to my desk. But no sooner had Mother left and than he would point that threatening cane at me as a warning to behave.

Good behaviour was not yet part of my vocabulary. I would revert to angry, frightful tears, jumping out of my wooden bench, running out of class past Safla Senior and chasing after Mother, all the while screaming "Bhabhi! Bhabhi!".

Yes, I called Mother "bhabhi", which means sister-in-law. It's what the rest of the extended family called her. I guess it just stuck.

As per routine, Hamid and Wahab – two Safla arse kissers from the senior class – would chase me, grab me by the collar, and taunt me with "bhabi bhabi".

The first time this happened, I knew I hated school and decided that I would hate anyone named Wahab or Hamid.

I also decided that I would show them up, by coming out first at school. Not because I was hardworking or intelligent or born with a higher intelligence quotient, but because Father would donate the ice cream on the last day of school.

AAG

The nerve centre – the kitchen – was located in a room at the back end of our house. It was a dark room, with a black cement floor, a black wall, a black ceiling, and a very black coal stove.

We could not afford a fridge. Sadly, we only consumed fresh meat and vegetables.

During those years, it was normal for each of us to get burnt by the stove.

The coal stove burnt Halima's long black tresses and she resembled a white schoolgirl with her short hair. Muslim girls were not allowed to cut their hair and Grandmother had a fit.

"You see what this modern country is doing to our holy customs! Next, they will want to go to school!"

Granny did not know that Halima was already attending school. She was secretly attending Ahmedia School on the pretext that she was learning how to knit and sew at dressmaker, Hafiza's, on Bristow Road.

After the accident Mother banned us from walking around the kitchen alone.

Once, while fiddling with the stove, Walla set his eyebrows alight. He ended up looking like one of those Chinamen.

I too, had my turn. I was told to fill paraffin, and ran out the back door with my head on fire. I knew then that I wouldn't want to be cremated when I died.

AHMEDIA SCHOOL

When space was finally available at a proper government-aided school, I stepped into a new world and into a solid red-brown face-brick building, in Bellair Road.

Despite being grateful that I would not have to endure those bastards Hamid and Wahab any longer, I was filled with dread. Mother would now leave me in the capable hands of Halima and Walla who would escort me to school.

I know Mother was secretly relieved that she would not have to endure my hollering every morning, but as she placed my tiny hand in Halima's, she would whisper into her ear, "Please take care of my baby."

Walla would assure Mother that she had nothing to worry about. But once we left Bristow Road and entered Main Road, my blessed siblings transformed into vile creatures.

"Your precious Bhabhi is not here now," Halima would say, with a pinch.The school itself was beautiful. There was a playground for the boys at the front. The soil was hard and red with two goal posts at each end. Tall pine trees lined the rough dirt road leading to the front gate. At the back were stepped, lush lawns with a variety of flower beds, and a netball area for the girls. Next to the school sat a mosque with a green dome. It had a fountain in front with goldfish and a green lawn. There were also some toilets alongside the river at the back of the school.

We wore white shirts, grey pants, green and white striped ties under a green blazer, and black shoes. Many children didn't come in uniform. Some came barefoot. No one was ever sent home.

VIDYA
If preschool was a ghoulish nightmare where I was regularly horsewhipped by Hamid, Hamza, Bilal and Wahab, all the while screaming "Bhabhi! Bhabhi!";

Class II. Butterflies , Roman Stentorians and Ustads. I am in the back row, 7th from the left (c.1954/5)

my first year at Ahmedia made me realise what a safe house Safla's had been.

My teacher was Mrs Roopram, a fat and friendly ma'am with a round Vyjanthimala-Marie-biscuit-type-Padmini face. She seemed to know what she was talking about. I understood some of it, especially when I managed to stay awake.

Whether it was boredom, an inability to grasp basic concepts, or because of sleepless nights from asthma and endless nightmares, I often dozed off at school.

A sharp slap from Mrs Roopram often disturbed my nap. I would open my eyes to find the rest of the class copying some impossible data from the blackboard.

C.A.T equals CAT
D.O.G is DOG
1 + 1 = 2
I SEE A KITTY
THE KITTY SEES ME

During the 1950s, Ahmedia permitted movies to be shown in their own hall at school. They even took learners to commercial movie houses like the Mayville Theatre and Albert Cinema. I saw Raj Kapoor's *Shree 420*, in 1955 and Cornel Wilde in *The Greatest Show on Earth* with selected learners.

When we saw the gripping love story, *Laila Majnu*, Mrs Roopram was seen wiping away tears. I think it was because she missed the last bus home to Dunbar Road and not because she just saw Shammi Kapoor and Nutan dying in a dust storm.

Back in her class, I always seemed to have problems keeping my pencils. I could never seem to find them when I most needed to use them. They would fall to the floor and roll off. And I would have to crawl on all fours under the desk. Falling objects have a habit of always rolling under other objects. And the rest of the class would always laugh at me. But I'd persevere.

I knew then, that without the cylindrical piece of timber-with-the carbon-lead in the centre, I would remain illiterate and dumb for the rest of my life. As I'd triumphantly crawl back to the bench of my desk, there was yet another challenge awaiting me. My brand new A5 square-lined exercise book, would now have disappeared. I'd catch the Omars, Khans, Moinuddins, Patels, Makkis, Naidoos and Jamallud-hens all around me, smiling. They were all guilty, meaning there was no one to blame.

Mrs Roopram, who sometimes wore a gold nose ring, was usually not in the least interested. She had forty other brats to worry about as she completed her mission statements for the day, on the chalkboard:

THIS IS THE HOUSE THAT JACK BUILT.
THIS IS THE MAIDEN ALL FORLORN,
THAT MILKED THE COW WITH THE
CRUMPLED HORN.
THAT TOSSED THE DOG THAT WORRIED
THE CAT...

But what about my pencils and exercise books and ruler that got milked every day, as they were tossed into thin air and made to disappear!

PYAR KIYA THO DARNA KYA

When Sumitra and Tara emerged from the Chedy house next door, all the boys from the neighbourhood would gather. They would even come from Dunbar Road, some five kilometers away.

The two girls, aged 12 and 14, would take their weekly walk down Carnarvon Road. On Good Friday they would take their cow, Gai, with them. Even my uncle from town would appear.

Tara was the elder of the two. She had a small round face, small, simple eyes, hair combed back with a middle path. She was starry-eyed. Her ambition was to become a film star in Bombay. Sumitra had better looks and locks, and seemed a lot more intelligent. She knew Bombay-dreams were silly.

Walla would gaze at Sumitra, and in his imagination offer her a branch full of half-ripe china guavas; which, even in his dreams, she refused to receive. When their parents got wind of the stir their daughters were creating in the neighbourhood, the girls were immediately locked up. They even locked the cow up.

Then there was Amina. She was a qualified teacher.

In those days, anybody who passed standard four was pretty much considered a professional. She hailed from an orphanage in 45th Cutting, across the river at the waterfalls. Walla tells me she was originally assisting Safla's school at Bristow Road, but had been poached by my father to tutor Hawabai after the stalking incident.

Amina was around sixteen years old. She was tall, dark and pretty.

It took Walla around sixteen seconds to fall in love with her. While this new tutor went about the business of teaching Hawabai the impossibly intricate mathematics involved in adding one plus one, Walla would sit innocently on the floor, slate in hand, acting very academic but being totally mesmerised by Amina's angular speaking profile.

When my father returned home early a couple of times and noticed this newfound passion for learning in Walla, he also put one and one together and gave Walla a thrashing, fired Amina, and banished Hawabai from even homeschooling.

And finally, there was this Kokni girl, Munawara. When she walked into our class, I was mesmerised. I had never seen a Kokni girl before.

She wore a lovely white dress, a beautiful striped green tie, a green blazer, white socks and black shoes. She had to. This was our school uniform.

Her long pigtails made her seem rather smart. Word got around that she actually travelled by train all the way from a village on the south coast, called Malvern. That means she took a steam engine to Berea Station and then caught a bus to Bellair Road.

I always wondered where Koknis came from. Someody said Cape Town. Others said they spoke Marathi at home and were from Cochin. I decided to ask Hawabai if we were allowed to marry Koknis. I don't remember what she said. And as I was mustering up the courage to talk to Munawara, she too disappeared from school.

JANNAT
In 1954, I found myself in a room diagonally opposite my class from the year before. My teacher was Mr Venketsamy.

Halima and other senior students had nicknamed him "Butterfly".

They were right. It looked as if he had just graduated from the larva and pupa stages, and got stuck. He would flutter around the hall with a short moustache and a short cane. In class two, I was introduced to the parallel dimension of Islamic education by grossly underpaid and underqualified 'religious teachers' called ustads. They wore a red or black fez with dangling tassels, a cane and a copy of the Quran. Islam was definitely not spread by the sword. The cane, now that is the more likely story.

Ustad always spoke in Urdu, the language of many Indian Muslims.

I understood nothing that Ustad taught, except the expression maar kow (take that). This was in the form of a smack from a cane on an open-palm, or a vertical whack on the head with a metal ruler. The cane came from the bamboo grown alongside the river behind the school. Every Friday, Sayed Moinuddin and Omar Khan were appointed to replenish worn out stock.

Learning to read Arabic was another nightmare. Images of Heaven and Hell were planted in our fertile minds. I would often ask my best friend, Yusuf Khan, to interpret and he would whisper, "Ustad is saying that everybody will be tried separately for their sins. If you see your mother and father about to be thrown into hell-fire, you will not be allowed to take their punishment instead. Up there it's going to be every man for himself!"

For me, heaven just meant no Ustad.

Standard 4 at Ahmedia School. Walla (first row, third from left) and Halima (second row, fifth from left) (c. 1951)

GARAM HAWA

Thick, hand-cut slices of brown bread smattered with raspberry jam, with a white enamel mug of hot, sweet cocoa at the first tea break was a daily feature at school. Lunch was varied. One day it would be mealie-rice and dhall, another day it could be peas and potatoes. Our favourite was genuine broad-beans curry. Although Mother religiously packed lunch for me for both the breaks, I would invariably join the crowd and dive headfirst into food really meant for indigent children. How was I to know that I was not poor? One morning at 10:30am, Osman loudly remarked after the first break, that lunch was being prepared early that day. When somebody inquired how he knew, he answered, "Because I smell curry." The boys – especially those sitting behind him – roared with laughter. It was not really the smell of curry.

It was actually a vulgar mixture of hydrogen sulphide and methane gases emitted by the backside of one of the big boys at the back, probably Bilal.

Osman's name changed immediately and forever to 'Curry Smell'.

SHAHEED

Our principal, Mr Ismail, was a real giant of a man. Tall, dark, always clean-shaven; he possessed the voice of a Greek stentorian. When he conducted the daily assembly in front of the school, I used to think his loud voice could surely be heard all the way to 2nd River. He was a no-nonsense Roman general. Hard and ready with a cane to take care of undisciplined grandchildren of the original canecutters, but also prepared to forgive and forget those who sincerely repented. He was very passionate and a shining example to his staff. Later on, he suffered a stroke and lost his voice.

But this story is really about Sattar.

My brother's friends decided to bunk school one day. Osman Arbee, Richard, Giddy, Walla and Sattar disappeared and headed towards Brighton Beach, 13 kilometres south of Durban.

Sattar was the uncrowned royal jester of the school. Always up to some prank, concerning either his best friends or the girls or even the teachers. Nobody ever took him seriously.

When they reached the beach and started swimming, Sattar began to scream and shout for help. Nobody paid any attention.

It was the last time he cried wolf.

POOJA KE PHOOL

Our Mayville house was located on Carnarvon Road. It had a corrugated length of about 200 meters and ran parallel to Waterfall Road, but on a much lower level. A stream that began in the direction of Randles Road, became a gushing river at times; fast and deep enough to drown in. It terminated in a scenic but intimidating waterfall which dropped towards Bristow Road and continued for a short way – mainly as pools – before mysteriously disappearing underground. I suspect it made its way to the Umbilo Canal.

A path ran down from Carnarvon Road to the river, negotiating itself with the other side across a set of slimy, slippery rocks and continued up a steep gradient towards Waterfall Road. This path provided a useful shortcut for travellers, from the lower Windsor and Carnarvon Road side of Mayville to the upper Waterfall Road end.

Halfway down this path there sat an odd-looking, half-rotten Tree with a hollow trunk and ugly roots gnawing their way out of the earth. About twenty Hindu devotees prayed to this Tree regularly, on Sundays and special holy days. They chanted mantras, burnt incense sticks, and decorated the base with tiny idols made out of clay and wrapped in marigold flowers. They left milk for the snake god believed to live inside the trunk.

I used to hide behind bushes and watch them, scared but mesmerised. Just before sunset, they would all suddenly rise and, in the blink of an eye, disperse and vanish across the river, up the gradient, and into the vacuum of Waterfall Road.

I would emerge just before nightfall and examine the remnants of their rituals. When the last golden rays of the sun began to slide off the trees and the birds began their dusky chirp, and the waterfall seemed to gush louder and faster, I knew it was time to go. But the Tree remained frightfully magnetic. I was seven. And hypnotised.

Something would draw me closer yet to this ferocious-looking creature. What was I seeking here at such a tender age? Despite warnings from both my brother and Mother about unexplained murders, hangings, suicides, sudden appearance of corpses, and equally sudden disappearance of live humans – all of which had occurred in this river-valley – I continued visiting it. It was as if I had to discover the secret of this sacred spot all by myself. However, the first sudden cracking of a twig, would sound like a thunderclap; clearly audible above the gushing stream, chirping birds, and the faint noise of the falls. This signal was my cue to quickly release the clay models, scamper up the pathway and head for home, never turning to look back because I knew there was definitely something following me. It was the 'bad wind'.

BHAYANAK BHOOTNI

Asthma. It never allowed me to sleep despite the medication. Father would prop me up in bed and plant a rubber hot-water bottle between my back and the wall. The heat would dissolve the phlegm in my chest, he would say. But when he turned off the lights, my breathing would slow. I would see a silhouette forming in the dark and moving towards me. It was the Tree. Only now, it had grown large, round, frightening eyes, that vaguely resembled my grandfather's. A deep vertical ridge resembled a nose, and a mouth with razor-sharp teeth. Branches that formed bruised and blistered arms reached out to grab me. This monster from hell wanted to crawl on top of me. Then there were cockroaches; giant, red, flying cockroaches crawling on the ceiling, their shadows suffocating me.

I'd get up and run screaming to Mother's bed. I'd be sweating, wheezing, sobbing, "Bhabhi!"

Mother would pinch me hard on my upper arm and curse me repeatedly for visiting that accursed, bewitched tree.

She knew that I had also wet the bed again. I always did, despite a curfew on consuming liquids after six.

She would remove the old sheet, wipe the rubber mattress protector and replace the sheet with a clean one. I'd receive another deep pinch, and be told to recite my prayers in that foreign language I was meant to learn at madressah. I was also warned to stay away from the enchanted forest.

SHENAI

The famous Mayville Theatre where American and Hindi films were projected onto great white screens, was not too far from our Ahmedia School.

At the time, commercial entertainment was banned on Sundays.

Cinema management would sometimes work around this and show "free" sneak previews on Sundays, as advertisements for their forthcoming attraction. One such preview was Filmstan's *Shenai*. It was released in 1947, but reached us around 1954.

I had never seen a film before. On this particular Sunday, I could see Walla making silent gestures to his friends, arranging to attend the preview without me. They were plotting to visit this new exciting thing called a bioscope. Father was fast asleep and I told Walla that either he could take me with him or I would wake Father up.

Of all the things Father hated, he hated being disturbed from a deep sleep the most.

Walla, seldom helpless as he was then, relented.

He cursed angrily and ordered one of his underlings to grab my hand as we all moved at breakneck speed out of the back gate, but in a direction completely opposite to the theatre. We all rushed past the Tree without even a glance, ran down the hill, along the stream, then climbed across the rocks on the side of the waterfall, into Bristow Road. A turn into Main and short walk into Bellair Road had us there in a matter of minutes.

I gasped, trying to keep up with the escort who had an iron-grip on my thin wrist, and realised that I had just learned Walla's secret shortcut to school.

Walla had heard the songs in this movie well in advance of its local release, and was not in the mood to miss out on his new favourite:

*"AJI AWO, MOHABBAT KE
KHALE KASAM, HAMARE RAHO
TUM, TUMHARE RAHE HUM..."*

*"Come, swear by your love that you will remain mine
and I will remain yours..."*

As we entered the mad darkness of Mayville Theatre, I saw shadows and silhouettes of millions of people against the silver screen. Housefull. It seemed everyone was there. Rajinder Krishan's lyrics dwarfed our petty thoughts and there was a mayhem to the excitement around. I glanced up at the screen as we walked. A giant ferris wheel rotated. Nasir Khan, brother of Yusuf Khan or Dilip Kumar, romanced Rehana.

*"ME DOL JAYE UPAR
ME DOL JAYE NEECHE"*

*"This carriage (of the wheel) moves up, as
That carriage moves down..."*

I was hauled towards the front rows of the cinema. Walla was visibly annoyed as we hustled for vacant seats. There were none. We sat on the floor, right up in front of the screen. We craned our necks to make sense of the characters on it. I was terrified and started crying and calling out"Bhabhi, Bhabhi!".

Even in the midst of cheers, song and dance, a prim and improper patron sitting on a proper seat nearby, picked up on my irritating, disturbing cries and protested loudly to my brother to "take that child home!".

Walla, eyes transfixed on the screen, prodded one of his serfs and commanded him to take me home.

The poor fellow initially pulled me out gently, but quickly gained momentum and virtually dragged me all the way home. There were no shortcuts back. It was all uphill; either via Main Road or the more aggressive albeit scenic waterfall route. He selected the latter, as revenge.

I stopped sobbing and paused to reflect. I had just seen my first talking picture and hated it. Walla also used the F-word on me for the first time which would be useful to blackmail him with one day.

RAMAYAN

Hindi-speaking Hindus immigrated to this country from Bihar, Uttar Pradesh and other north Indian provinces. They made the trip from Calcutta to become indentured labour on the sugarcane fields and so became known as "Calcuthias".

Peasant Muslims, also from different eastern and northern areas of India, came to South Africa via Hyderabad . They became known as "Hyderabadis". They also resented the term.

If the relatively richer Gujarati Hindus looked down upon the "Calcuthias" as lower caste, the Gujarati Muslims were also guilty of treating the "Hyderabadis" as inferior Muslims.

Next to our house at Mayville, there lived a large joint family of Hindi-speaking Hindus. Their surname was Chedy and their property was well below road level. They held a quadrangle of many single-storey buildings; some of brick and tile, others of brick and tin. Some housed sub-families, others were outside toilets.

Yet others were used as stables, kennels and fowl runs. This large family was a real collection of father, mother, sons, daughters, daughters-in-law, cows, dogs, fowls, and some grandchildren.

Red flags with Aum and trident symbols fluttered from very tall bamboo poles near the entrance. A makeshift driveway cut into the ground for cars, trucks, livestock and human traffic. An impressive temple on the one side of the quadrangle housed idols of Ram, Sita, Krishna and Hanuman. Milk was regularly left in a bowl to feed a reputed snake god said to live in the temple.

Quite regularly we heard screaming and shouting in what we understood to be Bhojpuri Hindi. Their complex was always surrounded by a cacophony of sounds. There were even fistfights, between husband and wife, and sister-in-law and mother-in-law.

Sometimes a drunk Thiluk could be heard telling his mother, "Ma, I will kill myself in the waterfall, then you will be sorry!"

Mrs Chedy would snap back: "And take that wretched wife of yours with you!"

On occasions, their entire complex would be wrapped in coloured lights and marigold flowers. A large marquee would be set up in the space between their complex and our retaining wall, and a stage set for some entertainment. It could have been a wedding, a religious ceremony accompanying the birth of a new child, or Diwali; any excuse to have some fun.

The entire neighbourhood was automatically invited, without frills or formality. There were no Muslims, Hindus or Christians here. There was no identity crisis or confusion. We were all simply Indians. Dogs were locked out of sight, fowls safely put away in their coops and cows locked away in their stables.

Ladies sat on wooden chairs, or squatted on the cold ground, wrapped in blankets when it was chilly. An invisible barrier separated the women from the men, who would be dangerously drunk by eleven o'clock.

Devotional poetry or bhajans would initiate the proceedings, followed by lighter forms of prayer and sometimes brief sermons by the pious.

Most of the people in our area were very poor. These simple celebrations brought people together to share their woes and joys while offering some hope to continue living.

Some very impressive dramas involving the saga of the sages through the ages, recounted the legends around the Mahabharata. A favourite told of the ordeal of Sita. She survived being abducted by the evil demon Ravana, was rescued by her husband Ram, then had to undergo a further humiliation; to prove her chastity.

These popular plays were the main course on the menu. Ladies would swoon over the actor personifying Ram. Men would drool at the sight of Sita dressed in a chaste-white chiffon sari, plastered with makeup. Bright red lipstick, white talcum powder, red rouge, orange-coloured sindoor in the centre-path of her pitch black hair, and a perfectly made dark-red sindoor at the centre of her forehead. As she made her way to centre stage, the chimes from the bells on her ankles could barely be heard above the din of the amorous catcalls from the gallery.

Few in their frenzy and lustful, drunken stupor, stopped to have a good look at her, or they would have realised that it was not a woman, but a man dressed for the part. They had forgotten that it was forbidden for women play themselves on stage.

There were some absurd comedies as well. My favourite, *Champa*, was about a newlywed bride who went against tradition and continued practising her Indian dancing when her husband and in-laws were away.

This tall, handsome male with thickly-lined kohl, false eyelashes, donning a black wig with thick pigtails (imported from India via Singapore) makes a sudden appearance from the left side of the wooden stage. She performs the Bharatanatyam to live music played by half a dozen musicians armed with a harmonium, tabla, dholak, and a bulbul tarang.

Champa is wearing a sari with gold sequins that reflect the coloured lights around the stage. As the music changes from classical to a faster, modern tune adapted from the popular movie Rattan, she abandons the Bharatanatyam and switches to swaying her hips. The younger men in the crowd salivate.

A burly male figure appears out of nowhere, and, using a club made of cardboard, strikes her down and places his heavy sandalwood jackboot on her face. The music stops just before he screams, "How many times have I told you that dancing is not allowed in this family?"

Champa sticks her tongue out, winks wickedly at the audience from under the boot and replies in Hindi, "Sirf sau baar" (Just 100 times).

This elicits wild laughter and approval, especially from the ladies. The unamused husband pulls out his wooden sandal and knocks it against poor Champa's head. The ladies do not appreciate this scene and protest by booing, jeering and waving their fists. Some young girls and boys throw small onions and tomatoes at the cruel husband. The men in the audience protest against the unruly behaviour of the ladies in the crowd. All this adds to the chaotic entertainment of the endless evening. I too, find all of this funny. Except the violence against Champa. I know it is make believe, but I have seen this scene enacted before, closer to home.

SHOLAY

'Daddy' was one of Walla's classmates. He came from a family of former indentured labourers. Most former indentured Indians remained extremely poor after their contracts as slaves ended. They held irregular employment or were left destitute. Daddy's daddy was unemployed most of the time, especially when he was between jobs at the Durban Corporation Solid Waste. They lived in a tin house, about five minutes' walk from our house.

Daddy had a younger brother called Abdul Gany, who had a peculiar squint. Though he was at least three years older than me, we were in the same class at school. He had no shoes, wore torn, dirty clothes and always smelt off-beat. We often walked to school together.

One day a copper penny falls from my short pants pocket. He grabs it, shouting excitedly that he has found money. When I protest that it is mine, Abdul Gany refuses to return it. Instead he punches and trips me. With two bruised knees, I go sobbing to Walla who is afraid of nobody except Father.

Walla is busy with homework but needs little excuse to abandon it. He drags me to Abdul Gany's house, hauling me by one hand while I scrape over the dirt track that is Windsor Road. We reach their tin shack and Walla shouts so loudly that the entire Mayville valley reverberates:

"MARAD HO, THO BAHAR OUE!"
"Come out if you're a man!"

I see Abdul Gany sneak out of the side door of one of the outhouses. It's a toilet and he has not washed his hands. No water. Also, no education.

He makes his way towards Walla knowing he can't dodge the executioner. They would, at some point, have to pass our house to buy a half-loaf of unsliced Bakers brown bread from the Rainbow Tea Room (which sells everything except tea). But instead of clobbering him, Walla instructs Abdul Gany to call his elder brother "Daddy" out.

As soon as "Daddy" faces Walla, my brother picks him up by his torn collar and belts him. "Daddy" falls backwards into a muddy puddle. His short pants tear.

"Walla, not "Daddy!", I protest, "Abdul Gany!"

Walla helps Daddy up gently and when he is upright again, delivers another cut to the jaw. "Daddy" falls once more. I am shocked, bewildered, and tug at the hem of Walla's also-short pants, asking him "Why?"

Walla glares at me.

"Do you expect me to hit Abdul Gany who is younger than me?"

MAUT

Abdul Gany has been absent from class for longer than usual. I finally corner him outside CN Rana's family store at the intersection of Bellair and Main. He is sitting on the edge of the pavement, his bare feet in the dirty gutter, clothes torn, as usual. He looks sad.

"What's wrong, Abdul?"

"We won't be coming to school anymore – my father died last week."

"Was he sick?"

"My mummy said he was 47 – old and time to die. My sister is on a wheelchair, so "Daddy" and I both have to look for a job."

It's getting late. Mother would be worried. Tomorrow is Saturday and no school. It's the day I usually add more rainbow-coloured grasshoppers to my collection in the postbox at the bottom of the staircase. I look up at Abdul Gany and turn around to go home.

The next day I spot him out of the corner of my eye and shout after him, "Hey! Where are you going?"

"To see my father. Do you want to come?"

I am seven. Abdul Gany is ten. I haven't understood death yet. I am not allowed to leave the enclosure of the house alone. Mother would kill me if I disappeared. Father would kill her if anything happened to

Grandfather Essa (c. 1955)

me. But I find myself following Abdul up the narrow path along Windsor towards Randles Road and before long, we reach the cemetery in Kenilworth Road.

'So, where is your father?"

"He is under here."

"Huh?"

"Under this sand. Deep – with God."

"Will he ever come back?"

"My brother says never."

"So what will you do?"

"Come here every day and wait. Maybe he will change his mind if I promise to behave from now."

I didn't see Abdul Gany or "Daddy" again. Days and months passed. Not at school, not at home. Have they all gone to join their Father in that garden?

DARR

I wake up one day in 1950 to find the house unusually quiet. It dawns on me that only Mother, Halima and I are around. Today I will not disappear to my favourite hideout and share my lunch with spiders. But where are Father, Hawa and Walla?

"They are gone to Transvaal. Your uncle Ismail is getting married this weekend."

"Where?"

"Carolina."

"Why are we still here?" I ask.

Halima explains that Mother is prone to travel-sickness. She doesn't tell me that Mother has been advised to stay home because she is expecting Ahmed in less than two months time.

I don't really understand words like wedding, marriage, travel-illness, or permits to cross the Natal-Transvaal border. But when Halima mentions it's Dingaan's Day – the day Afrikaners celebrate a victory over the Zulus at the Battle of Blood River – I feel a little scared. It makes no sense, but I am afraid. I am afraid that we are all alone and unprotected. I dare not leave the house today. Not even to the garden where I love to play with grasshoppers, or roll my tyre down the stairs.

I stand at the front circular window and stare at the massive lawn, with its pink and purple Christmas Trees in full bloom and perceive a scary, evil, silence, inching towards the main house like a dark stormcloud. I quickly move to a window in the lounge to find that the normally dense guava bush has suddenly grown wild and out of proportion. Some of the trees seem to have moved closer to the house.

I rush to the back stairs and stop just short of the kitchen. From here, I can see coal and wood piled in our backyard, the dusty parking area, and – further back – the forest with its monstrous Tree. In my mind's eye I can vividly see the waterfall plunging downwards. Only this time, the water is red. The corpses hanging from snake-like vines in this magic forest grow exponentially. Non-human forms resembling scrawny apes swing from branch to branch.

Above the roar of the falls, I hear a distant but clear beat of jungle drums. They seem to be getting louder, and when I cannot bear to hear or see any more, I rush back into the house, closing all the windows before the evil wind can enter. But I know I cannot prevent it from enveloping the house from the outside. I run to Mother and Halima in the kitchen, and plead, "Please lock all the doors and windows. Let's go into the main house!"

They are both busy and ignore me. I run to Mother's lap, pleading with her to sit next to me. And with tears and fears in my eyes, again demand to know, "Why are we left behind?".

GAON HAMARA SHAHAR TUMHARA

The endless empty space around the Mayville house complemented the dense bushes of wild guavas that never seemed to ripen. Father said they were bad for my asthma but I ate them anyway. The mysterious forest with its gushing waterfall, distant Sunday drums, and howling afternoon winds, hung over us like a full-time conspiracy. We still loved the place. It was the only place we knew. Everything that ever happened, only happened here. It's where I learnt about tadpoles and leap-frogs. It's where I collected Creamline Milk bottles and multi-coloured grasshoppers. It's here that I figured out that garden postboxes didn't mean regular mail.

Then one day in 1954, after the morning verandah was swept clean of overnight dust and dried leaves, Father told us that we have to move to the city.

"Group Areas Act about to be passed. Different races will live separately soon. Separate development. Apartheid."

He says Mayville will be rezoned for whites only. The Indians here will have to go.

"How do you know all this? Have you received a letter? Is it in the news?" asked Halima.

Walla answered for Father: "You know Father… he just gets to know."

The trucks are loaded, the house emptied. Only memories and some unused wood and coal remain. I am too bewildered to cry but Halima and Walla seem gutted. After all, this was home. It was here that our nearest and dearest neighbours – the colourful, cultural Chedy family – forever reminded us that we were Indians and not Arabs, with their dramatic concerts alternating with real-life strife. There was Michael, who lived across the road. We were best friends until he stopped lending me his red and white tricycle.

Then, there was our verandah which could turn into a white winter wonderland once we emptied out the whitening cream from thousands of aluminium tubes.

The daily dose of Naushad's melodies from Rattan, Dard and Dillagi emanating from the Witch's hut; permeating through the tall trees and thick grass, dodging all obstacles and ever-so-successfully reaching their target – me.

I remembered when Walla hid some copper wire belonging to 'Andy's Scrap Yard' intending to 'resell' it to them and referring to it as 'recycling'. He got caught with his short pants on, and received an electrifying, bare-legged lashing with the same copper wire.

As we shared the front cabin of the borrowed pick-up van, I asked Walla if we would return when this "problem is over". He said "never." And I wondered, "How does *he* know?"

We made our way slowly through puddles, out of Carnarvon Road and into Randles. I tried to swallow as much of the scenery as possible – the house, the trees, the neighbours. We continued into Ramsay

Avenue, past the tollgate bridge, into Berea Road and finally down into Alice Street. We finally stopped at 141 Grey Street.

Once all the furniture had been hauled up the one flight of stairs, I tugged at Mother, tired, sleepy, confused, angry and hungry.

"Bhabhi...when are we going home?"

"This *is* home. We are here."

2

141 GREY STREET

In 1920, passenger Indians from Gujarat jumped on the Saurashtra Express at Rajkot, then disembarked later, in Durban.

The wealthy ones quickly seized Pine, Brook, Albert and Prince Edward Streets, termed the Grey Street Complex.

The remainder became servants, or tenants of the zamindars, or landlords, sheepishly continuing with their previous, miserable, slavish traditions that had persuaded them to leave the Motherland.

The Gujaratis were either Muslim, or Hindu, occupying mainly Victoria and Prince Edward Streets.

The Memons confiscated Queen Street. Non-entities were shunted to the godforsaken areas of Cross, Bond and Short Streets, whilst sub-humans ended up in Carlisle and Lorne Streets. Fair-skinned Anglo-Indians hid in narrow Saville Street. They were discovered fifty years later and booted out.

Grey Street was alive in those days. Business thrived. Apartheid 'protected'.

All shops in Grey Street were men's outfitters, except G.C. Kapitan, opposite our flat. He sold bunny chows. Passenger Indians became rich businessmen, poor and indentured Indians, their customers. Shops never closed before 7pm on Fridays.

Although I had left a waterfall of nostalgic memories behind in Mayville, our Grey Street balcony gave us front-row seats to another world.

APNA DESH

Town was less than 10km away from Windsor Road, but the city felt so far away from the rustic, acrophobic environment of streams, green bushes and forests of Mayville.

The previous tenants of our flat had also been Indians. They had vandalised the flat with careful vindictiveness and were six months in arrears with the rent. They had also vanished overnight. It was back to basics as we all pitched in to restore our new home to a former, fictitious glory.

"Upar makaan, neeche dukhaan", or "house upstairs, shop downstairs"

Both our neighbours, the Arbee family to our left and the Bassa family to the right, fell into this category. Their shops were located directly below their residences. A passage from the Grey Street-end led to a flight of concrete stairs, which gave direct and only access to the three flats, built side by side, and all facing the extremely busy street.

The main iron gate to our flat, opened out to a small courtyard. Six-feet-high bricked walls separated the three flats. To the right were separate bathrooms and an oriental, low-pan toilet. Directly ahead of the main entrance was the clothesline area. A door led to the main building, which opened out to a dining area on the left and scullery on the right. Opposite was a small kitchen.

What immediately caught my attention was the balcony overlooking Grey Street. The house at Windsor Road opened out into a verandah that showcased the Mayville valley; with Kinfauns Road, Bristow Road, Jan Smuts Highway, and Bellair Road. This balcony's many windows were like a giant 3D-cinemascope screen which gifted us entry into a vibrant and dynamic alternate universe.

If you stood at the window facing Grey Street, you would see an amazing confluence of two entirely divergent cultures meeting at Pine Street, which separated the same single street into the Indian-dominated Grey on the left and the narrow-minded white-dominated Broad Street on the right. Shops on the Indian side were the famous 153 Bassa's, Narans', Minora Stores, India House and A.K.Ganie's - all on the same side as our flat. On the opposite side were Dominions, I.C.Shaik, G.C.Kapitan and Jhavary's. On the white side were numerous furniture stores, most of them owned by the Beare Group.

The famous West Street, the pride of the White section of the city, accommodated household icons like OK Bazaars, Greenacres, Payne Bros and Woolworths. I recall talk about single-decker trams – or buses-on-tracks – running through certain streets. These caused some hassles and were replaced by double-decker trolley buses. This mode of transport serviced the major maze of the white section of the city, running through Smith, West and Alice Streets. They also ran along the prestigious Whites-only beachfront, Marine Parade.

The trolley-bus service also had a line from the city centre that ran along the steep gradient of Berea Road, all the way to Jan Smuts Highway, and to the foothill of Bellair Road. These were for the white children living in the city who schooled in Berea, Essenwood, Manning and Musgrave Roads.

Apartheid dictated that Indians were permitted only at the front half of the upper deck of the red-and-white buses. Black Africans were confined to the so-called Green Mambas. Walla said that all services – banks, postal, transport and schools – were duplicated to keep the races separate. Some services like Home Affairs were even triplicated. The red-and-white trolleys soon ran into the red and became unsustainable white elephants.

MAA KI SHAKTI

Moving from Mayville to Grey Street wasn't good for me.

Some of the medication I was taking to treat my asthma made me want to pass urine regularly at night. To avoid Mother's ever-increasingly-painful pinches, I was forced to get up out of bed and relieve myself. Reaching the toilet was the problem.

I had to open two doors, switch on three lights, and walk alone across the cold courtyard, where garments left overnight on the clothesline became the banshees straight out of Macbeth. Only then could I reach the filthy closet, which my mother absolutely knew housed djinns or evil spirits or both.

Sorry, Mother. I prefer to take the pinch instead. So I am about to pee in bed when I feel a squeeze on my upper arm. Mother is not Mother for nothing. She forcibly yanks me up, follows me all the way through the graveyard of ghouls, makes sure that I wash up properly, and carefully tucks me back into bed.

DES PARDES

On some Saturdays, when no authority was around, Walla and I would climb onto the tin roof to have a mini picnic.

We would carry a paper-packet of oily bhajias, buttered-bread sandwiches (smooth machine slices courtesy of Kapitan's Vegetarian Lounge), a glass bottle of Coca-Cola and a pair of binoculars.

Whilst munching on the parapet of the half-rusted-to-hell tin roof, Walla would itch for me to start questions about the dozens of Indian businesses below us. Saturday mornings were very busy as government offices and schools were closed. Everybody went shopping except the enslaved indentured Indians who were now contracted to other, richer Indians; businessmen who expected them to be on 24-hour call duty.

"So Walla, tell me about that Jhavary's jewellery shop," I would begin.

And the know-it-all brother would reply, in between large swigs of high-pressured Coca Cola gas, "That was airlifted from Jhavary Bazaar, in Bombay!"

"What about Patel's Vegetarian Lounge?"

"Patel and Kapitan are from Gujarat. Sweetmeats and bunny chow are their specials."

"Why 'bunny'?"

"Banya, actually. Just a caste name for businessmen from India."

"Where did the mosque come from?"

"That is apparently the biggest in the Southern Hemisphere – whatever that means – and is styled on the famous Jumma Masjid of Delhi."

"Walla, look at those hundreds of ladies in saris. Explain that?"

"They are mostly from Madras. Those are Kanchi-puram saris."

"Who are the owners of the sari shops?"

"Mostly passenger Indians from Gujarat."

"What's 'passenger' Indians?"

"The first ones came as contracted slaves, to work on the sugar cane farms. The Tamils were mostly hired by the North-Coast estates whilst the South Coast, strangely, contracted mostly poor Hindi and Urdu-speaking people from the North of India! Passenger Indians came on their own."

"What is that brownish-red building straight ahead?"

"That is the Durban Central Railway Station. Look through the binoculars and tell me what do you see?"

"Wow! So many tall fir trees on Commercial Road and Pine Street!"

"EB, those are Pine trees. Now you know where that street gets its name!"

I am now getting bored and move the binoculars to the right – the forbidden White Zone.

"Tell me something about the whites on the right. Make it interesting."

"The fucking wit-ou's are stupid. They called our side of the street Grey Street and theirs is called Broad Street!"

"Why Broad?"

"The narrow-minded bastards! The only thing that's broad is the width of the emptiness between their ears."

"Why don't we find Indian shops on their side?"

"Group Areas. Separate development. Apartheid. We could trade anywhere before. Now we have to vacate. News agents like Burma House and Brilliant House and even the great Bombay Bazaar in West Street will, very soon, have to move!"

"But we can shop there?"

"You may shop where you like. Money has the same colour. But there is a limit. You cannot stay at white hotels for any amount of money!"

"What about Black people?"

"Shit! They have it much worse than us! They are not allowed to stay overnight in any city in South Africa."

"What about construction workers, maids, etc?"

"They have to be legally registered and issued a special permit. Both the boss and the slave can be imprisoned!"

"Walla, let's go down now. It's getting too hot. And how come you know all this?"

"By listening to Father. Next time, maybe shut up and listen."

BIJLI

Walla's encounters with electricity didn't end with the copper wire theft and resultant bare-leg beating in Mayville. Once, he buried a battery underground, attached a couple of wires to a bulb some distance away from the hidden cells and then went on to mesmerise his moronic friends with a magic light show.

Another time in Windsor Road, Walla stood on a table and very cleverly inserted a nail into the live socket in the wall. He received a nice 220V shock and fell off the table. My granny, relaxing on a sofa near-by, also went into a shock on hearing Walla's sudden thud. She coughed up red gunk on to the floor. Thankfully, it was just paan.

Walla received emergency attention when my grandfather returned home that evening. After a tiring and frustrating day's work at the tomato-box factory, he went on to box Walla.

Then, there was the incident in Grey Street.

Walla once asked our Uncle Mohammed for some technical advice to improve our radio reception. In addition to his interest in cinema, comics, and giving me a hard time, Walla also like to listen to cricket commentary, and followed the adventures of Jackie McGlew, Hugh Tayfield and Trevor Goddard. His white Gods as I liked to call them.

Uncle Mohammed was a master at doing extraordinary things in a hurry. Grabbing a pair of pliers and a roll of bare copper wire, he told Walla to follow him to the roof of the flat. There he rolled out a volley of instructions to Walla.

"Walla! Follow what I'm doing. It's easy. You don't need this. Cut it off. Shorten this. Connect that. Wait, hold this. Okay, join this."

Walla's eyes followed my uncle's instructions and quick hands. He was transfixed with admiration. I know what he was thinking: "GAWD! I want to become a Mohammed-bha when I grow older."

While I was thinking: "I want to become a Walla."

"There! It's done. Now you will be able to receive broadcast not only from Lords, but from Mars!" Uncle Mohammed said, smiling.

The roof of our house was already like a mini-substation, with its entanglements of wires and connections. When these two were done it resembled a major one.

That evening, Walla tested the radio. We returned with crystal clear news from BBC. Also, wonderful commentary describing the wicket and Captain Peter May's duck at the first ball.

Walla grabbed me, pulling me out of bed and away from his "Walt Disney's Silly Symphonies" which I had stolen from his side while he played with the radio.

He forced me to dance with him. He praised God, Mohammed bha and technology. And rejoiced at our joint success at this most complicated engineering feat on the roof that afternoon.

We made so much noise that nobody heard my mother complaining and swearing about the bathroom lights not working and the iron being out of order. We didn't hear the Bassa's the next morning complaining that their geyser had stopped working and that the cold water taps were now mysteriously giving off generous bouts of electric shocks. The cricket commentary was perfect. That is all that mattered.

BHOOT BANGLA

141 Grey Street of 1954 had it all. There were flats, warehouses, a printing press, and even a proper cottage on the Cathedral Road end. On top of shops that faced the street sat the creepy-floored Jummah Hall.

The wooden floored hall was used as a gymnasium for wrestling and boxing training on weekdays, and for weddings and concerts on weekends. There was a period in which it was used for ballroom dancing lessons.

My uncle's friend, Runga, offered such a class and I could hear the tap-tapping of feet on the wooden floor and the swish of couples as they practised through their fleeting steps. Sometimes I watched the bobbing heads through the shards of broken glass from our flat. All sounds – be they music or the shrills of gymnasium instructors – would come to a close around 8 o'clock in the evening when the hall would fall into darkness.

It is 9 pm. Time to go to bed. Have to rise early to catch the 7:10 am Green-Mamba to Ahmedia School. That is a long way to commute. I hope I don't encounter any wheezing attacks tonight.

I close my eyes, and the ballroom music begins all over again. I have not fallen asleep yet, so I am not dreaming. Walla is propped up comfortably on his own bed, reading an Illustrated Classics comic all by his selfish-self. "Hey Walla. It's that music again!"

And Walla, somewhat irritated at being disturbed from reading Les Miserables, answers casually: "So what? I have explained it to you a dozen times already!"

But I insist that he explain it again.

"It was this young woman who could dance as well as any professional but pretended that she was a novice, just so that she could be close to Runga's young, handsome, second-in-charge. She was in love with him, you see?"

I asked: "So what was the problem? Was she married already?"

"No, but he was!" Walla replies.

"Two years ago, her corpse was found at the back-end of the hall. No clues, nothing. Stabbed, strangled; I am uncertain."

"And what has all this to do with the music?" I asked.

I knew Walla would come up with a new story tonight. He was a master at changing the facts, as fictitious as they may have been. It was precisely why I never tired of listening to his bullshit.

"When Runga leaves at 8pm, she returns to the hall and continues dancing. Okay. Come with me!"

And I would follow him like a puppy to our bedroom window, which opened out to the dining room area, which in turn, faced the Hall.

Walla would ask me to be quiet and observe carefully. Through both these windows, I would watch as a light accompanied by a constant musical note, bounced off the walls. It would appear and reappear. And then disappear completely.

"Those are floating candles. She is teaching all the ghosts of past students who aspired to learn but died along the way!"

By this time I was too afraid to ask any more questions and begged Walla to please take me back to my bed. It was a long way off. Perhaps two yards.

Once there, I would cover my head with the cheap, dusty Swazi blanket and begin my nightly wheezing as I tried to block out the eerie music inside my head.

NAUKAR

Walla was in charge of buying periodicals which arrived from London's Fleet Street by ship every

Walla working out how many shirts I would need to iron before he allowed me to read Mutt and Jeffs. (c.1958)

week. These included *Tiger, Lion, Beano and Dandy*. Visiting newsagents, Brilliant House, on Broad Street, made Tuesday afternoons worth looking forward to. Some of the more violent comics were banned by the government. They were afraid it would 'disturb' their segregation policy, and 'influence' Black South Africans. Each week thousands of books and pamphlets were burned. It was said that hundreds of other periodicals were left to rot in Maydon Wharf.

Then there were some of the unlikely literary gems that came with the comics.

For instance, Green Lantern always began a new challenge with:

> " *In brightest day, in darkest night.*
> *No evil shall escape my sight.*
> *He who worships evil's might,*
> *Beware my power, Green Lantern's Light!"*

Or The Shadow's motif:

> *"Who knows what evil lurks in the heart of men? Only the shadow knows!"*

'Dell Comics are Good Comics' was the inspiring cover-page logo on these American dreams. Walt Disney's *Mickey Mouse*, Walter Lantz's *Woody Woodpecker*, and Terrytoon's *Mighty Mouse* were more than good reasons to survive those times.

I fell into instant slavery when images of this new art form fell before my eyes. I did not realise it then, but this craze would also introduce me to another form of human bondage.

My mouth would water as the bespectacled Afrikaner salesman rolled these pulp-fictions into the only reality I knew. But wait! I was not allowed to touch them, taste them or even smell from a distance. Walla made it very clear:

"Twelve Dell Comics plus a *Lion, Tiger, Knockout, Beano and Dandy*, right?"

I would nod, excitedly but nervously.

He would continue, "Ironing of one shirt and one pair of pants for each Dell daily. And shining shoes for the week for *Lion* and *Tiger*. Right?

I would try my luck, "Make it two weeks of ironing but school days only, and polishing shoes for two weeks only – for the lot, please?"

"Okay! But the *Mickey Mouse* annual will cost you an extra week of ironing!"

"What about the *Mighty Mouse* annual?"

This was Walla's cue to pull out the extra thick, published-once-in-a-lifetime directory.

"This one, brother, will cost you another month of ironing. Do you have the balls, baba?"

I knew Walla was a slave-driver. I knew this was not his own money. I knew he was capitalising wickedly on my weakness. As I grimly gave in, he must have clearly perceived but not cared about, the thought balloon above my comic head that read,

"Fuck you, Walla!".

SAAZ AUR AWAAZ

Nothing could prepare me for the new gadget my Uncle Mohammed brought to our flat one day in 1955.

He pants and heaves this wooden rectangular case – an electric plug dangling along the face of the stairs

– up to our flat. He asks Walla for the multi-plug and calls up a quorum; Walla, Halima, my Uncle Joosab from Carolina, and Father.

Uncle Mohammed opens the case, plugs it in, and loads a spool of very thin copper-coloured wire at one spindle, and an empty take-up spool at the other. A couple of knob-turns later and Mohammed Rafi's immortal voice engulfs the room:

"Tu Ganga ki mauji, meh jumna ka dhara…"

The song from *Baiju Bawra* (1952), he explains to his rapt audience, was actually coming from the very thin wire rubbing against a magnetic head. I didn't know what that meant and before I could figure it out, he nudged me.

"That's not all. Ebrahim, come and talk into this microphone".

He was talking to me!?

Uncle stops, rewinds, touches this button, that knob, and plays back my inconsequential chatter. I hear the most gorgeous voice over the solitary mono-speaker. It's mine! Everybody else has a go, including my Joosab-mama. He hums a song Father had taught him.

But Father is not very impressed. He wouldn't be. He had reportedly introduced, the first portable "transistor type" radio to his India village of Jodiya, so technology was not new to him.

"What else, Mohammed?" he says with some snarkiness.

Not to be outdone by his eldest brother, Mohammed instructs Walla to go to the Bassa's next door, and ask them to switch on their radio and adjust the medium wave band to a certain frequency.

The next minute, the Bassa family is listening to Naushad's magic and my family's voices on their own radio, through an illegal live broadcast. They too, marvel at Lata, lamenting:

"Bachpan ki mohabbat ko, dil se juda na karna."
As usual, authoritarian Father has the last word:
"Brilliant! Now get it out of my house before we all get into trouble!"

TALKIES

In sharp contrast to the quiet, open, farm atmosphere of Mayville, Grey Street was a busy, noisy city street complete with regular motor and pedestrian traffic. There was never a dull moment during the day. Madressa Arcade, adjacent to our building, provided a shortcut from the major bus terminus – called the 'Bus Rank' near the Indian markets – to the city centre.

Town was home to skyscrapers, bazaars, banks, post offices, City Hall, Central Railway Station. And near many other employment opportunities, like the ever-busy harbour and Maydon Wharf. But all the bustle bombed out at about 6pm.

Exciting radio serials like Tarzan, Superman, Captain Silver and the Sea Hound and Mark Saxon would all find a place to hide at about 7.30pm. So boring. So Walla invented regular visits to the cinema. The Avalon – at the corner of Albert and Victoria Streets – was our usual choice every week. Even if we had seen the movie before, the ever-changing chap-

ter of the thrilling, balanced-on-a-knife-edge serial
would make certain that we attended every Thurs-
day.

We sat at the same seats, B9 and 10, and bore wit-
ness to how Don-Daredevil escaped from the croco-
dile pit that he had fallen into last week; through the
trap-door, activated by the cruel-villain Dr. Satan. Or
how Zorro stops the moving-wall from crushing him
after Don-del-Oro's men had forced him into a corner
of the illicit gold mine.

Walla provided admission money. I made sure the
tickets were booked on time and that the penlight
torch was in proper working order. We needed it after
the evening show to negotiate the dark and narrow
passage to our flat after 10pm.

Walla, always the noble one, made me enter the dark
passage first. He had studied Aladdin's uncle, Jaffar,
very closely and learnt some crucial survival tactics.

When Walla felt I had the balls for it, we would
venture into the realm of High-risk Cinema on Saturdays. High-risk, because of the violence, not just on
the screen, but off it as well. Whilst standing in the
queue for a ticket, we'd be sjambokked by bouncers
who appeared to have graduated from asylums.

At more peaceful times, we would even try the
Hindi movies showing at the Albert.

Many motion pictures I saw, made a lasting impression on me, and caused me to develop a habit of
relating some events in the movie directly to reality.

JAAL

In *Jaal* (1952), Dev Anand is a villain who pretends to
be in love with Geeta Bali, but is actually using her

to smuggle some gold from Goa to Bombay. Geeta Bali is heartbroken and betrayed when she discovers what Dev is really up to. I remember whispering to Walla what a great singer Dev Anand was, as he tried to seduce the lovely, naïve native Goan, Geeta Bali. I was quite surprised when Walla whispered back that it was not Dev Anand at all but a playback singer, Hemant Kumar, who was dubbing-for-Dev. I looked up at the rectangular holes leading to the projection-room at Albert Cinema and thought: "What a talented fellow this projectionist must be."

But the real betrayal was yet to come.

Since Hawabai got married, it was decreed by the in-laws that she was no longer allowed to go to the cinema. It was tradition, we were told. But when she was on holiday at 141 Grey Street, we found a way to smuggle her to the cinema. On this particular trip, my newly married sister Hawabai and her sister-in-law came along for the film.

For some reason, Hawabai's sister-in-law felt the need to tell her parents that we had taken our sister to the cinema. Hawabai was immediately summoned to headquarters in Sparks Road. She was found guilty and her gate-pass to the city and our home was suspended for six months.

DAAG

In *Daag* (1952) – Dilip Kumar playing an alcoholic – carries life-saving medication to his ailing mother. But he is too late. He can't save her.

An unimaginably melancholic scene follows. The hero gazes in abject sadness at the partially moonlit

Hawabai preparing to sing a solo after her gate pass to the City was canceled (c. 1954)

sky, with dark clouds hanging about absolutely still, as he introduces a prelude to a timeless lament.

As I watch this morbid scene, my mind wanders, "How will I be able to endure Mother dying and disappearing forever, one day?"

SHREE 420

When Raj Kapoor's *Shree 420* (1955) came out, Ahmedia school in Mayville decided to leave the pious plains of rural Bellair Road and take us to Albert Cinema to watch the film.

"MERA JOOTHA HAI JAPANI
YEH PATHLOON ENGLISH THANI
SAR PE LAL-TOPI RUSSI
PHIR BHI DIL HAIN HINDUSTANI"

"My shoes might be from Japan, my pants English, and hat Russian – but my heart belongs to India"

I didn't understand the connection with the plot, in which Raj Kapoor tried to unwittingly scam the homeless and the poor into some non-existent housing scheme. But the socialist and egalitarian Charlie Chaplinesque sentiment resonated.

Also, these films and the others I saw later in my life, only served to entrench one central obsession; I would one day seek out the magical city of Bombay.

DOSTI DUSHMANI

The famous Indian Views press was in the same complex as our flat in Grey Street. After each edition, staff would discard blocks of lead used in the printing process. Guess who was the first person to discover this treasure, intercept it, and sell it to Father's scrapyard in Queen Street?

I would make 20 or 30 pence; a sizeable fortune for a nine-year-old pauper like me.

I invited my best friend and classmate, Yunus, to marvel and gasp at my newfound source of income.

Needless to add, I never saw the precious metal ever again. Yunus lived in Milton Road, in the Warwick Avenue triangle, light years from Grey Street. How did he manage to intercept the lead before me? Anyway, for wilfully helping himself to my rightful legacy, I did not want to talk to him again.

Although we were now living in the city, we still attended Ahmedia School in Bellair Road.

Indian girls, especially Muslim, were not encouraged to go to school until the late sixties. Halima was forcibly removed at Standard Four. Walla and I commuted to Mayville, from the city using Durban Corporation buses. We continued schooling at Ahmedia for two reasons, I was told. First, we had left Mayville during the middle of the year, and second, there was a shortage of schools for Indians in the city centre.

At Ahmedia School, hot cocoa was served at 9:30am and lunch around 12:30 daily. Each class had a stock of enamel mugs and plates which needed to be washed before and after meals by a predetermined, rotating pair of pupils. My partner was, of course, Yunus. But after the serious lead embezzlement episode, we decided to separate our seats and refused to accompany each other to the taps outside. Because we had not appointed suitable replacements to wash and serve the drink in time, there were severe delays in the cocoa-distribution network.

Mrs Roopram was informed that her favourite pair of young, handsome, fair-complexioned pas-senger-Indian-personalities were not good buddies anymore.

She smiled calmly and beckoned the class to sim-mer down, whilst the cocoa continued simmering up, outside. She looked our way, still smiling, and signalled with a nod of her Marie-Biscuit head for us both to come to the front of the class.

Yunus and I were the champs. I was a master of English, Yunus good at Maths. We were model stu-dents. She loved both of us. As we proudly reached her table, she removed a long cane from the top of the cupboard and, still smiling sweetly, casually asked us to bare our bottoms.

She raised her cane.

"Master Essa and Master Shaffie. You do have a choice. Hug and make up and this will all be over!"

With the normally lecherous Patel, Hoosen, and Omar-Khan boys, and the abnormally lecherous, Paruk, Lockhat and Makki girls so wide-eyed, gig-gling and impatient for action, Yunus and I jumped off the table and lunged towards each other like two Hajibhais.

AMAR KAHANI

Between Grey Street, Soldiers Way, Commercial Road, and Pine Street, lay Nicol Square. Political rallies of the day often occurred here. It had also been a trading post, and a parking lot for horse carts and farmers' trucks. Because of the fiery protests against apartheid held here in the fifties, it became known as Red Square. The outer parameters of the square consisted of a smattering of tall pine trees, but they flattered to deceive, for this was an empty, dusty square. But from my point of view, from our flat in Grey Street, the entire square was a forest. As far as I was concerned, Nicol Square was the enchanted forest I had left behind in Mayville.

If Walla told me about Robin Hood and Little John, the feud and friendships in the streams of Sherwood Forest overfilled the city's gutters. If Halima read Little Lulu and narrated the story of Old Witch Hazel brewing a wicked batwing brew, I saw purple smoke rise above the Payne Brothers skyscrapers.

Back at Ahmedia School, where, in spite of being very weak at arithmetic and famous for spilling ink all over with my G-nib, I was still the uncrowned king of storytelling.

The path to the throne had not been easy and meant stealing Walla's comics and from his treasury of classics like *Treasure Island*, *Kidnapped* and other abridged stories.

I was blessed with an uncanny memory to remember only the only important thing in life: fairytales!

Whenever staff and pupil absenteeism was high – which was more the rule than the exception – and classes were combined, it stood to reason to call upon the ace who would keep these packed classes busy with stories, even if they had heard them a million times before. And did these poor pupils care if I added my own variations?

To localise the action, I would relate the tale of *Goldilocks*, but this time around, she stole porridge belonging to the Nagaria family in Wiggins Road, across from the school. Snow White continued eating apples as red as her cheeks, but would instead be poisoned by that old, wicked Mango-Auntie who often released her two black Alsatian half-breeds on poor, innocent scholars trying to help themselves to the ripe mangoes that had fallen from her trees.

Midas, meanwhile, merrily converted base metals not into gold, but into precious lead before selling it to scrapyards like Father's.

Slowly and surely, I would shift the location of these stories to my newly discovered green forest in the city.

Next time I narrate the timeless tale of *Jack and the Beanstalk*, I would put my foot down! No silly Mayville landscapes would be used as background. When the Giant decides to chase Jack, our hero's uncertainty about which tree the villain was using to make his way down to earth, forces Jack to cut as many pine trees as possible. All those lovely green sentries disappeared from the city landscape.

And this, of course, explains why nothing remains of our original forest at Nicol Square.

SAMUNDAR

Walla and I shared a close bond. We were always united. Especially when it came to being jealous of our kid brother, Ahmed.

Ahmed had a white and red tricycle while we had nothing in any colour.

He seemed to obtain everything on a plate. This three-year-old brat would cry on most Sundays after we had just had our breakfast of weak tea, dunked with plain white Bakers' bread.

"Mummy! Mummy! I want to go to the Bay with my bike. Tell them to take me!" And Mother would reply calmly "Don't worry. Why do you think I gave birth to your big brothers? Finish your breakfast my baby and change."

I would exchange glances with Walla and whisper "Is that why I was born? You told me the reason was to serve you and iron your clothes for the rest of my life!?"

Walla would whisper back and wink at me "You leave it to me. We will sort the brat out."

As I carried the heavy tricycle down the stairs followed by the heavy Ahmed, I would wonder which brat Walla was referring to. When we were about to leave, Mother would advise us from the top of the stairs to be careful how we crossed the streets and even at the last minute, enquire whether we would manage.

Walla, always the smarty-pants, would reply, "Mother. Don't worry. It's just Pine, Saville, West, Smith, St. George and St. Andrews Streets, and Victoria Embankment and some silly railway tracks to cross. It's not such a big deal."

These were among the most dangerous roads in Durban. This is where apartheid was at its most vicious. Here, cheap white delinquents would thrash any coolie in sight.

Walla and I took turns to stand on the rear axle of the tricycle and push it forward fast. Ahmed loved his black curls flying backwards as he felt the wind in his face. Whoever was free would dish out the roasted peanuts and sweet popcorn that we bought from the one-armed, basket-wielding vendor, using Ahmed's Sunday money.

Shame. Ahmed was too busy enjoying the ride to notice that we two were greedily chewing up his weekend allowance.

On reaching the Embankment, Ahmed would order us to take him across the railway lines to get a closer look at the water in the bay.

We had to carry the trike down a long flight of stairs that led to the subway between the Embankment and the bay.

It was a mysterious underground passage, similar to a bomb-shelter. There was nothing mysterious about the ever-fresh stink of urine all over the concrete floor, despite signs in many languages –including Chinese – that warned against causing any type of nuisance here.

Sometimes, when the passage was flooded due to blocked drains and heavy rains, Walla-the-engineer would guide us to use the safest method of crossing the railway lines. No, not directly across the tracks. He claimed his method was far safer. "You cannot trust these harbour trains. A goods train can appear from either side at any time. Follow me!"

So we would climb onto the roof of the subway building carrying the tricycle and Ahmed, and carefully crawl under the clumsy hanging cables until we reached the other side.

It was not our fault that nobody bothered to warn us that the cables carried a very high electrical tension of about 13200V.

The promenade was built of concrete but had an iron railing at the water's edge, especially built to prevent exuberant Ahmed from riding his mini mean-machine directly into the bay. Ahmed loved

Mother keeps Ahmed and I at close range whilst Father is away in India. (c. 1954)

feeding the fish and asked for the packet that he had reserved for this purpose.

"Where are the nuts?"

"What nuts? EB ate them along the way."

It was then that Ahmed would kick up a tantrum and cry, "I will tell Mother when we get back home and tell Father when he returns from India!"

As far as three-year-old Ahmed was concerned, India was as far as Rossburgh. Being seven, I knew much better. It was further. Closer to Clairwood.

Sometimes – when the tide was out – we would walk over to the Maydon-Wharf end, and, like messiahs, walk on the seabed of the bay!

Ahmed loved nothing better than to play with the fossils, crabs, mussels, dead-fish, live-fish and especially some delicate, brown, irregular sausage-shaped object.

"Ahmed! Don't touch that shit! It's dirty!"

But Ahmed would turn the other cheek and become more cheeky.

"Goo! Goo! Baby want goo!"

Walla would then politely administer mild corporal punishment and slap him on the wrist, all the time guiding him out of the unholy water. I was always full of intelligent questions,

"Walla, how come that pipe is bringing that dirty stuff straight into the bay? Won't the fish eat it? And won't we eat the fish and therefore eat our own shit?" Walla was always full of smart intelligent answers, "You ask too many stupid questions!

3

91 ALBERT STREET

It was 1956. The eviction notice we had been served had come into effect. They were building a new passage from Grey Street to Cathedral Road called Ajmeri Arcade. It was time to go.

We had to leave Grey Street.

This was where we had been introduced to high-class cinema, weekly movie serials, Dell comics, Runga's haunting music and azaan from the Juma Musjid through the cacophony of the crowd below.

It was where we had battled to cross the busy Grey Street intersection, absorbed the inimitable aroma of GC Kapitan's bunny chow and enjoyed adventurous walks to the Durban bay.

The move would never be anywhere as traumatic as the loss of the Mayville home but maybe it was because we were moving to Albert Street; around two corners and three short blocks away?

Grey Street had offered few friends. And one villain in Yunus, the heavy-metal thief. In sharp contrast, Harwin Court at 91 Albert Street was saturated with sidekicks of all ages, religions and languages. Christians that spoke Gujarati, Hindus that spoke Gujarati, and Muslims that spoke Hindi, Urdu, Memon and Gujarati. These languages and religions belonged only to parents. My friends only under-

stood one common language English, and only one mean-
ingful religion, fun! Soccer on Friday nights, carrom-board
tournaments on Saturday evenings, Policemen-Robbers,
Hide-and-Seek, cricket, Monopoly, billiards, Cowboys-
and-Crooks, athletics, movies and ghostly-storytelling on
Sundays.

BHOOL

Early morning walks to Pine Street to catch the bus to
Ahmedia School in Mayville were becoming increas-
ingly difficult. Father enrolled me into Anjuman Islam Primary School in Leopold Street, a stone's throw
from our Albert Street flat.

It was so close that on some days, I would laze in
bed till I heard the first school siren, then cover my
head and go back to sleep, till I heard the second and
final one.

On being enrolled into Standard 3 I landed a seat
next to the window. The empty spot next to me was
ultimately filled by the last pupil to be enrolled that
year. Kantilal Mistry was gawky and tall, much older
than me, wore thick-rimmed spectacles and was a
dark-looking Gujarati. Mistry used to ask me to help
him with his school work. But I had a problem with
Mistry.

His face was a minefield of infected acne. And he
had this habit of picking at the pus-ridden sores on
his face and then touching my book, my ruler, my
pencil, even me. I could not handle it. I finally begged
Father to do something about this new problem in
my life. Soon after, Mr. Chetty discreetly asked Kantilal to swap places with another boy, Abdul Sattar.
I don't know how the swap was explained to him,

but when he gathered his things, there was a pained rejection in his eyes.

It didn't take long before a new evil replaced the old. Newcomer Sattar was obsessed with Shammi Kapoor and would go on to ask me if I had heard the latest numbers from the superstar. Whenever I replied that I hadn't, he would go on to sing-screech it to me in a voice that almost had me scratching at my own skin.

SHOOTOUT AT LOKHANDWALA

We had lived in sweet harmony with other Indians in Mayville, those days. Before the Chedy family in Windsor Road, there was the great Bhana dynasty in Main Road. They were our immediate neighbours in 1949.

By the time we had moved to 141 Grey Street, and later to 91 Albert Street, I had all but forgotten about this family. Until one day, when saw a lovely brand new, white Chevrolet Bel-Air whizzing through Albert Street in all its eight-cylindered glory.

Mohan – my best friend who also happened to be Gujarati – was the first to notice the magnificent vehicle and its tall, handsome driver. He was quick to excitedly exclaim "Hey! That is Keshu Bhana! Their outfitter's shop is next to Kapitans in Grey Street! Rich people!"

That's when it all came flashing back

The Bhana Family in Mayville, when I was barely five years old!

To outdo Mohan, I responded, "We know them too. They were our neighbours!"

Not that this helped me in any way.

So it happened on one afternoon in 1958. We were playing Cowboys and Crooks on the pavement in front of Kathorian Trading Company on 89 Albert Street.

The crooks, led by the evil Kaushik and the devious Dalsuk, had imprisoned my gang in a den – the staircase at Bobat Building. I had to free them because I was the only surviving cowboy. Kaushik ('Cowsick') would execute them soon with his cap pistol and run off with the loot that my gang had stolen from the bank.

There was no honour among thieves, those days. Sailesh ("Saila") happened to be passing by, having just offloaded a parcel ("potla") of saris for his father into the 1953 Blue Morris-Minor.

Traditionally he was always part of 'their' gang. This was my big chance. I jumped at him, twisted his arm behind his back, holding my ivory-handled-made-in-England-Sheffield-Steel toy gun at his poor head.

"COWSICK, release your prisoners at once or your vegetarian brother is DEAD MEAT!"

I could just imagine myself, like heroic first-grade actors John-Wayne in *Stage-Coach* (1939), Tyrone Power as The Gambler from *Natchez* (1954), Alan Ladd in *Shane* (1953) or even B-grade actors like Roy Rogers, Gene Autry and Alan Lane.

Kaushik and co. had no option. Sailesh was definitely one of 'them'.

They obliged and put their guns down. Everyone, except cattish Kiran, who dived for my brother Ahmed. All hell broke loose. A free-for-all fracas ensued. There were fists and bullets in the foreground and loud music in the background.

Top: The Brothers Mohan and Dalsuk in the midst of a serious fallout.

Right: Mohan: "This episode will make the gunfight at OK Corral seem like a Sunday picnic". (c. 1956)

I dashed across the road without a much as a look-left for traffic. This end of town was quiet on week-days and dead on Sundays. Except today.

There was a loud, sickening screech of brakes as a car bumper just missed me. I fell onto the tarmac and looked up. It was the Bel-Air and *Keshu Bhana*.

It was, to be more accurate, Mr Keshav Bhana! I knew this man! Father also knew his father and grandfather. He kept his car running. It was a flu-id-drive, forerunner to the fully-automatic.

Keshav stepped out of the car. As he helped me up, I found myself shouting, "I know your family. I know your family. You are Keshav Bhana. They call you Ke-shu–" As soon as I stood up, he gave me a tight slap.

CHOR

CTC Bazaar, a huge department store in West Street, had a bargain counter for toys that had been broken during transit from Japan, and sold for less than half-price. I was always the first to arrive at the counter every month to grab the best damaged electrical cars, train-sets and robots, among other stuff.

At Anjuman, Yusuf Khan, my best friend in stan-dard 4, once asked me how the broken-toy-bargain-worked.

"Yusuf...the toys are reduced. I buy them and take them to pieces!"

"You mean you actually fix them?"

"Who said anything about fixing them? Most times I can't put them back together and end up ruining them altogether! But it's really fun to try."

So Yusuf, already deciding that I was mad, issued a challenge,

"What else do they have on that counter that's not electrical?"

"What are you after?"

"Swimming goggles"

"I know goggles. How much must the price be? Like maximum?"

"I want you to get it for me for nothing."

I took this challenge most seriously.

"Okay, I will do it," I finally replied.

That very afternoon I found myself browsing through the latest consignment of toys on the clearance table. There was everything except a pair of goggles. I felt let down. There had to be another way.

I paid for the metal robot, marked down from ten to three shillings because the battery cover was missing and it had a random wire sticking out.

The cashier – an old white Afrikaner lady – recognised me, smiled and packed it in a C to C Bazaar branded paper bag. Instead of leaving the store, I went to the sports section upstairs and finally found them; a pair of red-brown, quality goggles for fifteen shillings.

Honesty, integrity and morality all went out the window as I calmly opened my packet and slipped the goggles in. I was sure nobody had seen me. I hoped so.

I walked briskly towards the exit. Nobody had ever stopped me before. I would get away just like that. Yusuf Khan would know that I was not just a city-slicker but a real slippery city slicker that would make the Artful Dodger look like an amateur.

"Can I examine your packet?"

It was the old, uniformed security guard at the exit. A thoroughbred Afrikaner. They were all thoroughbred. My mouth was in my heart. How could I have been so stupid? What would it be? Robben Island? Detention without a trial? Early morning hanging at John Vorster Square in Pretoria?

Then by some divine intervention, the sweet cashier's voice interrupted, "It's okay Andrè. He's paid for the toy."

I could not help hearing the last of her words with the guard as they watched me walk out. "He's a good Indian boy, that one. Very clever. He fixes all these broken toys. Really smart!"

I walked out feeling like a real arse.

USTADON KE USTAD

Mr. Imam was our religious teacher at Anjuman School in Standards 3 and 4. He was an amateur boxer and a passionate fisherman. He taught us Arabic and Urdu, in English. Between his tall stories, eccentric recollections of fables from the Far East and the Arab world, and his exploits in the ring, he actually managed to teach us some very strong moral and religious values.

Once, on a quiet weekday, Yusuf Khan and I gatecrashed the Saptah Mandir – a Hindu temple in Prince Edward Street. We pushed through the unlocked door, overturned a few Hindu idols and broke some marigold flowers hanging on the upper doorframe. We were proud of ourselves. We had done our bit for Islam. Damaged infidel symbols. We would enter heaven one day. Directly.

We decided to proudly relate this great deed to Mr. Imam. He would shower us with admiration. Give us

Class of Standard 4 securely flanked by two of the best teachers ever! Mr Imam (left) and Mr Rowley (right). And oh, I am sitting next to Mr Imam (c. 1958).

his blessings. Encourage us to go to Andalusia and join Salahuddin Ayubi's quest to conquer Europe.

"No, no, no! How could you do this? After all I taught you? Where did you get this evil idea from? Respect all religions! Absolutely! What you have done is a sin! Ask Allah to forgive you and don't ever do it again!"

Unrelated to our story; Mr Imam died shortly thereafter. Clearly there is no space on earth for good, honest people.

Finding good, English-speaking vernacular teachers was just as difficult as locating bad English-speaking vernacular teachers those days. So Anjuman employed an old man "Sayed Saab" from Riverside.

His English was poor. I suspect so were his morals. I sustained the best-quality hiding from him, mainly because I could not understand a word of Urdu. Sayed Saab became my nemesis. I began to hate attending school, and when Father picked up that something was wrong, he confronted me.

"He hits me daily! Because I don't understand what he wants of me. He speaks only Urdu!"

And Father asked me to describe this new devil.

"Thin, tall, white beard, long woolen overcoat, red fez…comes from Riverside Mosque."

My father stands up. "That bastard."

"If he is who I think he is, no more mosque classes for you at Anjuman."

"But why?"

"He apparently axed somebody to death. Leave it to me. I will sort it out tomorrow."

Father immediately arranged an audience with our principal, Mr. Khan, and informed him that should there be no other class for me to join, I would no longer be attending religious classes.

"Mr. Patel, please don't overreact. Everybody gets their fair share of corporal punishment nowadays. It's not really that bad," Mr Khan says.

Father got up and raised a finger to his mouth, "Mr. Khan, can you read my lips? I want him OUT!"

"Out is right. If he does not do religious classes, he will have to find himself another school!"

Father shook hands with the principal and whispered, "Please expel him immediately, if you can. And before you do, check out the laws governing government-aided schools."

A few hours later, Mr Moola of the Anjuman Trust visited Father at the shop in Prince Edward Street. He had come to convince Father to change his mind.

"What do non-Muslims pupils do at Anjuman during religious classes?" Father asked. "WHAT DO NON-MUSLIMS DO AT ANJUMAN?"

"They just hang around."

"Well, let Ebrahim *also just hang around*."

And that was it. For better or worse, I stopped attending mosque classes forever.

GUNAHON KE RAASTE

After the phenomenal fallout from Islamic lessons, I was exempted – not without some duress and evil eye – from all religious tests and examinations. *I loved it*.

It was midterm exams in 1958. Whilst the rest of my class would be writing Deeniyath (a subject dealing with basic Islamic knowledge) after lunch, I was free to leave at noon.

I was about to leave through the side exit of the school, when two of my best friends (everyone was my best friend) Ebrahim Madaree and Sayed Ahmed, on prefect duty, confronted me.

"Hey EB, where do you think you're going?"

I replied almost arrogantly: "*Saturn Satellites and Missile Monsters* – a super double. Last show today at Avalon."

Anybody who observed five-times-a-day prayers back then was deemed a fanatic, and I knew there was no point in trying to convince these two die-hards, so I greeted them and left. But Madaree grabbed my satchel and demanded to know more. "What are those films about?"

I reply like a geek.

"From what I hear, the first of the double is about the natural moons of the planet Saturn, which have been invaded by aliens from a distant galaxy that has now ceased to exist. These moons are their new temporary homes. An earth-mission to Saturn during this same period is met by violent hostility from the aliens..."

"And the other one?" asked Sayed Ahmed.

"Something about aliens from Mars that launch rockets to earth but these rockets transform, on landing, into horrible creatures..."

Wide-eyed, mouths salivating, Deeniyath notes in hand, Madaree winked at Sayed Ahmed: "Dawood Ustad won't mind, Ahmed. We are his model students. He would never fail us. It's only a silly June exam."

They debated the issue for a few minutes, with Ahmed stuttering loudly in front of some other pupils that the whole idea was crazy. A couple of

My brother Ahmed and I (c. 1958)

minutes later and there were ten of us in the queue at Avalon. Sayed Ahmed was right in front. We had pooled all our resources. He volunteered to book the seats.

And what exciting power-packed action movies they turned out to be!

Black and white, third-grade, low-budget, back-street Hollywood junk; absolute magic.

At interval, we all converged at Avalon Tea Room. A Baker's snowball and a bottle of coke for each of us put us back about five cents. The rush at the café posed a challenge equal to, or more violent than, any alien invasion. We scrambled in for the second feature.

The sets, costumes, and even the actors were the same as the first show. Cheap bastards! We loved it!

The films ended at about 4:30pm and we parted ways. I would now go home and boast to my brothers Ahmed and Walla how I had convinced my best friends to miss their exams. I would also boast about the exciting double-feature they had missed and which had just been taken off the circuit.

Shame! I love it when Ahmed and Walla are sad.

The next afternoon, I report to them about another exciting double feature. This time at school.

Madaree, Sayed Ahmed and the others, who put deadly martians ahead of mandatory, morbid madressah, would get a serious reprimanding and a zero for Deeniyath. The first feature was directed by Dawood Ustad, the head of the Islamic department.

After interval, the second feature occurred. Mr. Khan lined all the guilty ones outside his ground-floor office, called them in one by one, and dished out the neat lash of the cane on their halaal hind-

Ahmed (middle) smiling after receiving Diwali fireworks from Pravin Gordhan (left) and his sister (c. 1957)

sides and handed them a first-and-final letter of warning, for their parents to sign.

Both Ebrahim Madaree and Sayed Ahmed later agreed that both pairs of double features were well worth it.

AAG SE KELENGE

The garage next to our block of flats at Harwin Court, 91 Albert Street made us nervous. We worried that one day, some inconsiderate idiot would carelessly start a blaze in the garage and turn us into sausages.

It was Diwali of 1958, and as usual we would obtain a whole pocketful of fireworks for the festival of lights from Father's commercial partner Mr. Jamnadas Gordhan. His son Pravin would deliver them to us.

While others were quite content to launch sky rockets from coke bottles and observe from a distance, or light Big Bangs and run, I was a little more daring.

This Diwali, I would demonstrate how rocket power could be used to propel sea vessels. I attached a Devil Chaser to a paper boat and floated it on a pool of stagnant water outside a blocked gutter alongside the petrol station. I knew that the boat would be carried across the pool like a flash. If you snoozed, you would lose the opportunity of witnessing an amazing, once-in-a-lifetime event. I signaled Ahmed to even call Maharaj. He was the garage manager and a petrol attendant. And a tyre repairman, cashier, bearing puller and toilet cleaner. Such a nice man.

He would reward me with a raspberry lollipop every time I successfully called that young, Tamil-Christian auntie from flat four for him. Her real name was Poobathie but everybody called her Ruby because her eyes sparkled on a pitch-black face.

In the split-second between striking the match and lighting the fuse, somebody should have reminded me that the smelly, stagnant water outside the garage had been contaminated with flammable diesel, petrol, motor oil and Maharaj's high-octane urine.

The flame rose ten metres high, higher than the roof of the garage. I was not really worried. Maharaj was a nice man. He would not scold me, even if both the garage and Harwin Court were razed to the ground. So long as I called Poobathie for him, he would be happy. But trust a police car to be patrolling past at that precise moment.

Before they could stop; Mohan, my brother Ahmed, my cousins mini-Ebrahim and I, dashed into Harwin Court, the gutter blazing behind us. I think to myself, Maharaj must handle this. He is the manager after all.

Mohan ducked into his flat, while Ahmed, Mini-Eb and I entered our home, looking for places to hide. Mother was in the kitchen at the time, frying samoosas. Sensing the ruckus in the bedroom, she came over and asked why Ahmed was under the bed and mini-Eb inside the closet.

"Ebrahim burnt the garage. Ebrahim burnt the garage!" Mini-Eb screamed.

Ahmed and I deny the claims.

"But please don't open that door if anybody knocks. Tell them we are all gone to the mosque," we say.

We hear our Mother screaming, "Oh no, it's all burnt. All of it is gone!"

I am terrified. Sitting in the darkness of the cupboard, Ahmed whispers to me, "What will they do to us now?"

We finally crawl out of the cupboard, biting our lips and stunned into silence, when Mother enters the room.

"The samoosas are all burnt! Bastard children. Wait until your Father gets back!"

I was relieved. Father would take some time to return. He was still in India.

ZORRO

Moosa Meer, Fatima Meer's father, ran one of the oldest Indian newspapers in South Africa, Indian Views. His office was first at Ajmeri Arcade and then on the ground floor at Harwin Court in Albert Street. The newspaper was also renting Flat 6 as part of its activities in the building.

A man far ahead of his time, Moosa often got himself into hot water. His newspaper was anti-colonial but it also tackled issues within the Muslim Gujarati community. The newspaper eventually moved out in 1958 and three families moved in. A boy named Farouk, who became known as "Flat 6 Farouk", also moved in. He also became a best friend until I discovered his dark side.

I had just watched the Tyrone Power version of Zorro in 1959 at the Avalon and was so carried away by the action that I decided that South Africa also needed a Zorro of its own. After all, there was so much injustice here as well. I could visualise it now:

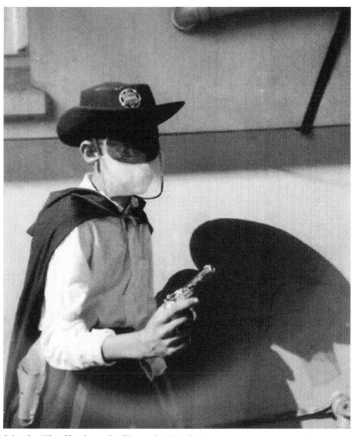

Me aka The Shadow aka Zorro (c. 1958)

The Masked Marvel, the Don amongst the downtrodden, the Sultan of swashbucklers, the leading lariat amongst Lash LaRue's.

But I had to prove myself by becoming the Zorro of Harwin Court before I could be recognised nationally, so I called up an emergency meeting in Kiran's flat.

Following the arrival of Sailash, Mohan, Ahmed Gora and Dalsuk, I made the announcement.

"I have just been appointed Zorro of Harwin Court, any objections?"

Kiran seemed to have one, "Who appointed you?"

"By the powers vested in me, I pronounced myself Zorro," I said with a flourish.

"What do you mean you are Zorro?" Ahmed Gora asked.

"It means you are all villains when we play Cowboys and Crooks. I will always come out the winner. What I say goes. Any questions?"

Within two days, I had my sister Halima design a black cloak for me with a "Z" made out of white bias-binding tape. I bought a long-sleeved black shirt from Jacols' Wholesalers, a cowboy hat from Greenacres, a black holster belt with silver studs and two silver pistols with synthetic ivory handles from Payne Bros. I made myself a mask from my old hardcover general science notebook. Zorro was born, and rode out of flat 16 at full gallop, straight into a legend.

The next Saturday, I met up with Mohan-and-them at the staircase next to Aunt Khatija's flat. I asked Ahmed to take roll-call. Everybody was there at the pre-appointed time. Everybody except "Flat 6 Farouk".

"I wonder where he is. He has never missed a meeting before!"

"So, Zorro, what is the plan?" Mohan asked me.

Today's plot would be as follows: my younger brother Ahmed, who recently complained that his name always featured last in the credit titles of our activities, would be a captive, guarded by villains Dalsuk and Kiran.

Mohan would play Zorro's close ally – the deaf and mute Bernardo – and when he gave a signal, I would slide down the dangerous bannister, feet first, alight on the landing with my glorious cloak flying high behind me. A crack of my lasso at the imaginary chandelier above the villain's head, brought it crashing down. Within seconds, I would flatten all the overweight Spanish buffoons, employed as guards only to catch votes, and take care of both Kiran and Dalsuk in a fancy fencing duel, fatally wounding them both. Meanwhile, Mohan would cart the weak-eyed Ahmed to safety. Finally, Zorro would jump on his white horse, allow one loud bray, tip his hat to all the Spanish female admirers most graciously and ride into the sunset. Boy! I could not have written a more perfect script.

So why was Bernado hesitating to give me that all important signal?

Why hadn't the game started?

"What are we waiting for?" I ask.

Everybody pointed to a dark figure standing at the 2nd floor end of the staircase. Time stood still. The evil shape stepped out of the darkness. The stranger seemed very familiar. He had a Zorro outfit identical to mine, except his lasso was longer.

And then "Flat 6 Farouk" spoke up.

"Are you blind? I am the real Zorro!" he thundered.

I was angry. This brat was spoiling my show. My friends would lose respect for me. The fickle fools!

He lunged at me with his wooden sword. I fought back, swinging at him and exaggerating the play with my lasso. He broke my plastic sword in one swipe and laughed. My two shillings sword from Victoria Cycle was no competition. I managed to grab hold of his wooden sword and jumped on it, cracking it through the middle. Before we knew it, two masked boys were throwing punches at each other while rolling down some concrete stairs. The gang prodded us on.

The fight only ended when Mohamed Bhai, living in Aunty Khatija's flat 18, grabbed us by the scruff of our cloaks and demanded we stop fighting with each other.

We did. And we all got to join Zorro's legion after that, wearing masks, fighting injustice, just as Moosa Meer had done with the pen.

JUNOON

I was born to read. If nothing else was available, even the telephone directory would do. At others, a quick walk to the library on Brook Street opened a world of excitement for me. I loved Enid Blyton – especially the Adventure Series.

It was always the same gang in all the stories. This was a relief because it meant they would all survive for the next book.

All these stories had a common start. It would be Christmas or summer holidays, when the young adventurers arrived at their cousin's house – usually a farm for their vacation. Their Aunt Caroline would serve them a sumptuous breakfast; hot farm porridge made from homegrown oats, dashed with Uncle George's pure honey from his own apiary, eggs collected that very morning from smiling, enterprising hens, and finally tea or coffee, with hot milk from the farm's own cows. The breakfast was complete with the freshly baked bread slathered with butter or marmalade.

Everything made sense – porridge, eggs, bread, butter, milk, but I had never heard of marmalade.

What was it? I had to know. I had to taste it! But how? I battled to evoke an image of this exotic substance. It even gave me insomnia. When I saw a collection of glass bottles on display in the window of Patel's Cafe on Prince Edward Street, labeled Rose's Marmalade, I got my first look at the jam. It was on special, too. One shilling and sixpence.

I went crazy like a dog in front of a butcher shop. But behaving like a mad dog would not score me a bottle of this adventurous stuff. I was broke as usual, so I appealed to Walla and Halima to help me out. They were always there for me. Honest and true. They both said no.

I decided to confront… no, not Mother. She never had any money. In fact, none of her dresses even had a pocket for small change. She carried a tiny purse on Tuesdays only, to buy vegetables from the morning market. Mother would ride a rickshaw back home and use the change to tip the rickshaw-puller, Bhengu, who helped haul the heavy carbohydrates and mineral salts, loaded in a wicker basket and paper carrier-bags, up the three floors of Harwin Court.

She did not bother counting the change. Money had no value unless she spent it. That is why Father never gave her an allowance.

Back to the marmalade. Father seemed genuinely confused when he heard what I wanted.

"I hear it's very tasty," I said.

"But how do you know?" Father replied.

"Enid Blyton says the Adventure Team always has it for breakfast on the farm. And they love it. They even tell their aunt so!"

"Okay, but it comes out of your allowance," Father replied, shaking his head.

I grab the two coins – a shilling and sixpence – and go sprinting across nine steps at a time, reaching Patel's in record time. I proudly pass the loot to this friendly, chubby Gujarati, grab the bottle without even asking for a brown-paper packet, speed back home, twist the metal lid open, dip my finger in and take a taste of this divine, God-sent honey from heaven.

It tastes like shit.

Bitter. Ugly. Horrible. How could Enid Blyton – or any other blighter – do this to me, especially after I had loyally read all of the Adventure series?

But this story does not end there.

"So, my boy! How is the marmalade doing nowadays, eh?" Father asked after a few days.

I reply calmly, "Its nice. I can't put it down. Try some. You will love it."

Father seems to like it. "Father, you have been so good to me. Please. Have the whole bottle."

Within a week the jam's gone down Father's hatch.

Months later, I see the special is still on at Patel's. I politely enquired from the younger, assistant Patel, "So Patel Junior, how is the sale going?"

And he replied, "A bit slow, sonny. My father sold one bottle so far."

JUNG

Sometime in the summer months of 1963, I was on my way to the barber shop at Leopold Street when I heard the usual Daily News vendor frantically shouting: "Read all about it. The end of the world is near. The end of the world is tomorrow!"

I was very busy that day so I decided that I would read about it the following day, when the world had ended; the city-late edition would tell us how it happened.

All these newspaper vendors are the same! Did they think buying that edition would save the world?

Anyway, I was more concerned about getting this short-back-and-sides before school inspection the next day, or run the risk of catching some shots on my backside.

At Bob's Barber Shop, I found the usual irritating queue-on-the-bench. *How come these people got here before me? Don't they go to work? Didn't these students have homework? And how come there was nobody on the bench when I passed this spot fifteen minutes ago, on my return from school?*

Bob was ill that day, so his old, semi-retired partner Harry was attending to all the clients by himself. The radio above blasted irrelevant world news so loudly, that eventually I could not hear my own thoughts, so I decided to catch forty winks. Easier said than done; because in addition to that pesky radio, these nitwits around me, waiting their turn at the chair, gossiped louder than Marconi's noisy invention. The competition between rabble and radio was now reaching near-exploding point. Every time the gossip got louder Harry stood on a stool and turned the volume of the radio even higher, until he had it at full volume.

Then he lost it. He still had the scissors in midair and one hand on the shoulder of his contemporary client. "Shush gentlemen! President [John] Kennedy is about to launch an invasion on Cuba!"

The crowd stopped talking altogether and looked at each other. A second later, they returned to their petty stories.

Once again Harry went closer to the radio, struggling to listen to the details of the invasion. I concluded that his client would not get the usual high quality Tony Curtis cut today.

Again Harry put the scissors on pause, this time keeping his other hand on the clients ear-lobe for no useful reason whatsoever, then screamed at the bench:

"SHUT UP, you people. For God's sake! This is bloody serious!"

This time the crowd shut up. Each client grabbed a magazine and buried their heads. Some in shame, some in anger and most in self-pity. Only big-mouth Marie, who was not a customer but a small-time zol-peddler in Leopold Street had the courage to confront Harry.

"What's up Harry? What is the radio chooning?"

Harry shook his head. "Looks like Third World War tomorrow. And this time they are using nuclear shit. Remember Hiroshima? We are fucked."

It then dawned on me what was being played out here. If President Kennedy invaded Cuba, President

Kruschev of the USSR would, in retaliation, give the order to Castro to launch those nuclear warheads already pointing, towards Washington and New York. This would initiate a world war which would turn out to be the grandmother of world wars, and one way or another, signal the end of the world.

I realised I was wasting my time sitting in this stupid queue.

School assembly would be cancelled tomorrow. Surely there would be no uniform inspection either.

I am going to read my Spiderman comics again and have some buttered bread and tea for the last time, I decide. I go home.

TOOFAN EXPRESS

When we tired of the usual boyhood games on weekends, we would often call up a meeting to discuss the next challenge. Especially on a rainy Sunday and after a punctured football. We met in Mohan's flat.

Dalsuk spoke first. He had light brown eyes and a husky voice.

"Let's take a train to Wests. It's a railway station on the harbour line, near the Bluff."

"Yes. But what is there?" I asked.

Dalsuk said that next to the station, there would be two pathways. One leading to a view of town and another leading to a staircase that would take us to the lighthouse we could see from the beach.

"We can catch the train at 10 minutes to 12 and we can return at half four. It costs two shillings," Dalsuk explained.

It sounded amazing. We agreed. And Challi, from Navijan Court, got roped in too.

Durban Central Railway Station on Soldiers Way, like all other government entities, was another ugly symbol of Apartheid. All amenities were duplicated for each race. This included toilets, booking offices and even coaches. We appointed big-mouth Challi to buy our tickets from this old Afrikaner at the counter.

We stood nervously at a safe distance in total admiration of Challi's courage. The bespectacled Boer poked his head out of the mouse hole at the counter.

"Six half return tickets to Wests, please, sir."

"What will you be doing there?" the Afrikaner asked, lowering his spectacles to stare Challi in the face.

Challi smiled with his pretty, pink tongue sticking in between his teeth and politely replied, "We are going for an adventure, Meneer, sir."

"Ja! But better behave yourself on the train, eh!"

Challi returned with the tickets boasting how he had not been afraid of Meneer Malan, the ticket seller. He also claimed to have convinced Malan to give him the best seats on the train. But I knew what he was after. Challi wanted a permanent seat in our gang.

When we reached Platform 13, we found all the coaches were the same. So were the seats. Challi that bastard liar.

We rushed into the car excitedly.

Every station we passed was less exciting than the previous one. Dalton Road, Maydon Wharf, Rossburgh; all so quiet, such drab empty, plain white buildings. All so meaningless on this rainy Sunday afternoon. We reached Wests, and were the only ones to disembark. The station looked like a place where passengers go to die. We looked for the two pathways but found nothing. Defeated and hungry, we walked back to the station to wait for the train to return.

Needless to say, Challi and Manna were not granted membership into our gang.

MAIDAN-E-JUNG

In the early sixties, Leopold Street terminated in a cul-de-sac; a result of a new bridge that joined the previously disjointed Albert Streets.

The bridge eased traffic congestion in Leopold Street. It also gifted us a ready-made space to play soccer, easing our search for a soccer ground close to home.

Every Friday evening, our gang would pick sides and kick rubber balls till midnight, regardless of weather conditions – apart from electric storms.

Everything was perfect for years. Nobody bothered us except some unreasonable Winderfield Court residents who would complain to the police that we were disturbing the peace after midnight. Could we help it if the game went into extra time?

When this happened, the police would pick us up and drop us off at the beachfront or near the bay, and expect us to walk all the way home. So we did that. We would walk back to Leopold Street and continue the game exactly where we had left off.

We also had another set of foes, determined to have us leave the area and stop the games.

The notorious Leopold Street Gang insisted that since we technically did not live in Leopold Street, we had no business there. Chris, the leader of the gang, walked around with a vicious mutt and bullied us.

So I came up with a plan. I told Chris that if him and his bozos wanted to beat us, they could perhaps challenge us in a relay race instead. In some ways, the winner of the relay would win the territory; or so I imagined. Chris agreed to the race.

On Monday afternoon after school, and just before the race, we went through the plan.

Salee would begin the race at the cul-de-sac at the corner of Leopold and Albert Streets at 4:30pm, in front of the Kingsgate Clothing factory. He would pass the baton to Rugs at Springbok Tea Room Corner.

Rugs would give it to me at Hansa's Corner at the Prince and Grey Street intersection. I would run through Prince Edward Street, past the Raj and finally hand it over to Mohan, who would run along Albert Street and complete the race.

Only a city-slicker knows what a mad idea this was.

Salee knocked over a bricklayer near Anjuman School, just ten seconds after he started the race, Rugs rammed into dozens of bewildered people and their parcels, who cursed him on their way home from another thankless, underpaid, overworked day at the clothing factory.

As I grabbed the baton from Rugs, I heard somebody issuing a death threat to him. I quickly advised him to continue running in any direction but mine. Soon I was forcing my way through the patrons who had accumulated in front of the Raj, for the 5 pm show of The Ten Commandments – and finally passed the baton to Mohan, who did not really have to sprint too fast, as we were ahead by nearly half a block. We won by a mile, as they say.

We received loud applause from our supporters at the finish line. A whole five of them. We also got a good swearing from bystanders and pedestrians. Far more dangerous and violent were the threats from the rabble-rousers of the Leopold Street Gang. They accused us of cheating, claiming that Rugs lived in Soldiers Way, so we had no business using him on our team. Rugs was from Soldiers Way, so they were right about that. But we never admitted it.

The tension continued, but it wasn't long before Chris, his family and dog, moved elsewhere. It was just us versus the police now.

CHACHA ZINDABAD

Comic books were my life those days. As stated earlier, the more violent types like Superman and Batman were banned.

I once spotted an advert in one of the funnies:

SECRET ORIGINS OF BATMAN 50c
SECRET ORIGINS OF SUPERMAN 50c
COLLECTOR'S ITEMS
GIANT ANNUALS

SEND $1-00 FOR BOTH, POSTAGE PAID TO:
SUPERMAN DC COMICS,
575 LEXINGTON AVENUE
NEW YORK, USA

I lost all my sleep. I could not eat or drink or think. I had to get these books or die trying in the process. But they were definitely not available at the local

CNA or Tennyson Burroughs. Where does one begin with this mission? First, I needed to obtain, a US dollar.

I asked my father directly.

He thought I was mad but offered me some advice.

"It's not so easy. Go try Barclays Bank at the lower end of Smith Street." Having said that, he left for India once more. I went to the bank and the tellers all laughed when I asked for one. Finally, a white man felt sorry for me and let me buy one for 68c.

I put it in an envelope with a brief letter:

Please send Batman and Superman Annuals.
I enclose one dollar.
Thank you.

I sent it. When I thought about it later, I realised how stupid I had been. And if I hadn't realised it on my own, my brothers Wallah and Ahmed were determined to let me know how stupid I had been.

I also found out that the offer was for North America and Alaska only.

Mohan, Dalsuk, Kiran and Kaushik all made fun of me, too. Then my entire class.

Then, one evening, my uncle Ismail called me and said he had a packet for me at his place. "I picked it up at our postbox this evening."

It actually came. A packet of comics – collector's items! Superman and Batman all the way from New York. I could not believe it.

I paraded with it at home, at school, on the streets. I lent it to no one and didn't allow anyone to even touch it.

DEEWAR

It was almost Sports Day, and being useless at sports, I decided I would spend my time becoming a good spectator. But Mr Fulchand, my Latin-language teacher insisted I do something to boost the image and morale of Hussein House. Or serve detention.

So I drew a giant poster depicting an athlete belonging to Hussein house, reaching the winning post well ahead of the other athletes. I displayed houses Reddy, Sastri and Tagore all fumbling by the wayside and looking like idiots. Each athlete would say something sad and sorry about his own inability to keep up with the leader.

It was my first political cartoon, so I believed that it qualified for the student noticeboard at the entrance to the main building, called The Wall.

Most of the notices already pinned to the board were mundane timetables, rosters or inconsequential messages.

I removed all these useless pieces of paper so my giant poster occupied the entire space. I felt so proud, as every pupil making his way to the assembly area stopped, read my poster, and either laughed, praised it or made some unsavory remark under his breath. Staff members, their attention aroused by this unusual, unprecedented excitement at the Wall, also moved in droves to study the poster.

The next morning during class registration, I received a message to see the principal, Dr A D Lazarus.

I was ecstatic. I was going to be honored by Dr Lazarus, known as the first Indian matriculant, the first Indian graduate in the Arts and the first Indian to hold a PhD.

I imagined the praise he'd heap on me. He would ask me why I hadn't drawn a cartoon before. He would ask if my parents were artists.

As I walked in, Dr. Lazarus was rummaging through a pile of papers on his desk.

"Remove that rubbish from the wall immediately. This is your last warning. Who are your parents?" he demanded without even looking up from his table.

He waved his hand, signaling me to leave.

I was livid. And in tears. I pulled the poster off the wall and went home.

I looked at it. Without thinking, I made a minor adjustment and put it back on the wall the next morning. The revised poster drew more attention, more laughter, and more noise than the original. I obscured the cartoon by writing "CENSORED" diagonally across it.

Again, I had to report to Dr Lazarus.

This time he sat me down and looked me in the eye when he spoke.

"What is your surname, again... Essa?"

"Where did you get that idea from, Essa?"

"Rather ingenious, Essa. I must admit."

"Be careful with this government, Essa. You could be in trouble one day, as I am."

JEET

Sports Day arrived at Sastri College. Banners, flags, war cries, booing, cheering, teasing, music, marching and lunch packs – especially lunch packs – all added to the excitement as we made our way like Trojans to Curries Fountain.

After the buzz around my cartoon, I knew I had inspired my House to be completely victorious that exciting day.

Of course, none of that happened. We came out last.

The Invitation Medley Relay was the last event and the highlight of the day. Most high schools from around greater Durban would participate. The race had evolved, I was told, from the old postal system. Fast runners would chase down vast distances to pass on mail to the next runner. I can't remember who told me this, but the system was said to be a lot more efficient than horses. As the adage goes, all horses have rights while only some humans matter.

In this medley, the first runner would cover 880 yards (twice around Curries Fountain), the next two would sprint 220 yards each, and the final athlete 440 yards. This totaled 1760 yards or an imperial mile.

Although this was meant for just high schools, the "tribal college" for Indians, on Salisbury Island, also received an invite. It was no secret that it was not more than a glorified high school anyway. Other noteworthy institutions were Springfield Training College, the ML Sultan Training College and Gandhi Desai (both in town), and Bechet College in Sydenham, which was a school for coloured kids. Completely black and white schools had their own competitions.

Sastri College had very little hope of doing well because, apart from being up against the very best of Natal's Indian athletes (especially Bechet College), our own athletes were either fatigued or injured from the earlier events.

The highlight of the day's events finally began, and our first athlete began poorly, lagging way behind everybody else. He passed the baton to Cassim Abbas, our master sprinter, who recovered some of the deficit incurred by the first lout. This recovery was subsequently lost by the next runner. The baton was finally handed to our last runner, Krish Sewpersad, who had to cover the final 440 yards. He was in last position and over a hundred meters behind the first runner from Bechet High School.

Sewpersad was a real athlete; he had already been awarded the Victor Ludorum for his conquests at our school, but nothing prepared us for what was to come.

One by one, and as effortlessly as a hot knife through original Rama margarine, he overtook all six athletes ahead of him, and made his way closer and closer towards the giant from Bechet. Barely six yards from the finish line, Krish, our superman, overtook him to win the 1962 Medley for Sastri College.

The applause reverberated off Curries Fountain and promised to ring for a thousand years.

AROUND THE WORLD IN 80 DAYS

In 1956, Jules Verne's *Around the World in 80 Days* was due to be released at the cinema. Months before its release, flags were flying between the Avalon cinema and the famous travel agency, AI Kajee building. The cinema and the agency were on opposite sides of Victoria Street, so special permission had to be obtained for the decorations.

The storyline was simple. Hero, Phileas Fogg, takes a bet that he can travel around the world within 80 days, using all possible modes of transport available. It was thrilling.

After watching the film, I was so inspired that I walked straight to Springbox Tea Room and purchased a blank jotter for 3c. I then returned home, had a cup of tea with two slices of buttered bread, and began sketching my own, original, comic series: Around the Planet in 80 days.

Little planning, rehearsing, draft or rough copies of the storyline, dialogue or even the features of the characters was ever done. There was no time nor resources, so the first copy was essentially the final copy.

Using a ruler and a black ballpoint pen, I divided the page into six or eight rectangles, inserted the title, chapter number, drew the figures freehand, inserted the impromptu dialogue in thought or speech balloons, brief narration windows or time-dividers. I would end each chapter on a cliffhanger.

For example, our hero in my version of the comic, is almost a superhero. His name is The Falcon. He can fly but has no other superpowers. He takes a bet with an obnoxious millionaire that he can touch down on all the other eight planets of the solar system using a spaceship, and return to earth within 80 days.

The first chapter lands him on the moon and he immediately faces a challenge. A chemical contaminant on this natural satellite threatens to destroy a vital electronic component in his rocket engine. The exciting chapter ends with Falcon watching helpless as his ship disintegrates in front of him.

I never had any idea how these crises would be resolved when I drew them.

So when I distributed these serials to my classmates at school, or to my gang at Harwin Court, one chapter at a time, I'd get asked, "So EB, how will he get saved?"

To which I had only one answer.
"I will have to ask The Falcon how."

SHAHJAHAN

In 1961, *Ben Hur* arrived at Shah Jahan cinema at the northern end of Grey Street.

Word got around that Sastri College was organising an excursion for all Standard 7s to go and watch the epic. I had heard that special cameras had been used to shoot a chariot race between the hero and the villain, supposedly at the Colosseum in Rome. It also boasted a stereophonic soundtrack, screened with high-tech, modern widescreen projectors at selected cinemas.

The excitement lingered and expectations were almost painful. We would only get to see the film the following week.

Naturally, schoolwork took a back seat that entire week.

Money was collected from all the classes in record time. No pupil turned down this exciting offer, and any pupil unable to afford the fare would be assisted by the school fund.

But then something happened that killed our mood.

Exactly five days before the booking was finalised, our form teacher dropped a bomb.

"Bad news, boys! The principal has changed his mind. Only the History classes will be allowed to go for the film. Your money will be refunded."

The reason? Apparently it was decided that learners in the bookkeeping classes would not benefit from watching the film given that it was a historical film of Biblical proportions.

Bookkeeping was meant for learners who were destined to become straitjacketed clerks. Nerds. Low-life, linear nincompoops. Sub-human. And was what I was studying, obviously.

There were eight Standard 7 classes, and each class had an average of 30 students. Half of these classes chose History and the other half took Book-keeping.

We protested against the decision, but nothing worked. We suspected that this about-turn had not come from our principal Dr. AD Lazarus. We figured it must have been a History teacher who felt 240 students would be too difficult to manage.

Numbers had literally destroyed the dreams of bookkeepers. Well, at least we'd get jobs.

Later that evening, I narrated the story to Father about how the school had dashed our dreams. It was all so unfair, I said.

Walla, a commerce student at ML Sultan Technical College at the time, was busy as usual typing some homework at our dining table when he overheard my whining. He stopped typing and interjected without even taking his eyes off his Remington typewriter.

"*Ben Hur* may be biblical, historical, mythological or even *plain bunkum*…" he said. "But just go and remind your teachers that no film can ever be made without fully understanding the commercial viability, budget, and financing".

Father, who had been pretending to hold sympathy for my sadness, heard Walla's comment and smiled. At least one of his kids would have a future, I imagined him thinking.

The three of us put our heads together and within minutes had drawn up a polite petition, which highlighted in more detail what Walla had explained. He also typed the appeal. All the nerdy students signed it the next day and immediately submitted it to the office.

We won. And, needless to say, loved the film. And that we were in the front rows – seeing the film ahead of the those freethinking history students – gave us immense pleasure.

RAAT KE ANDHERE

Father was a very humble man. He had only two gold rings, each with an expensive diamond on his left hand. Being very fussy about the shine, he would dip them into old, spent, tea water. It helped remove the tarnish, and improved the shine.

One day – after afternoon tea at the shop – he removed the tea leaves from the teapot at the kitchenette in the back of Bombay House, placed them in hot water and left his two precious rings in the pot.

That evening it was reported to me that they were returning from an Indian movie at the Naaz Cinema and as they crossed the robot at Prince Edward Street, Walla asks Halima, "It doesn't make sense. How did Lalita Pawar know where the daughter-in-law had hidden the gold bangles?"

Halima explained, "That Lalita is a witch. She was spying on Padmini when –"

Before Halima could finish her sentence, Father – who was walking behind everybody else – suddenly accelerated, overtaking Mother and stopping her in the middle of the street. "What do you mean you threw the tea leaves into the bin?"

"This is what you do to old tea leaves," Mother answered.

"But you threw my diamond rings away?!" he raved.

"How was I to know?!"

"Didn't you check the pot?"

"I did not expect gold rings in teapots!"

Father was now losing it, after having lost the rings.

"Tojee jibree! Allah will cut off your tongue one day!"

I was busy with some maths homework when they all stormed into the house around midnight.

Within minutes, we were all jogging to our family shop two blocks down in Prince Edward Street.

Watching Hindi films those days was like attending a wedding,very elaborate.

Halima was still dressed in a sari, Mother in one of her better-looking floral dresses, and Walla and Father in suits and matching ties. I had to rush out equally elaborately in my pajamas.

We first checked the small kitchen at the shop, going through pots, pans, cups, the bin, the washbasin. We then opened the backdoor which had ten locks; enough to make one believe we stocked De Beers and not the imitation jewellery we were known for. We rummaged through drums containing tons of smelly garbage, broken plastic and glass bangles, and other discarded jewellery and junk from India; which collectively seemed destined to stay here forever.

Father was now using new Gujarati words on Mother. Mother, for her part, was learning new retorts.

Back row (left to right): *Uncle Ahmed, Uncle Ismail, Auntie Ayesha, Uncle Gani, Uncle Mohammed.*
Front Row: *Aunt Mariam, Grandfather Essa, Grandmother Heerbhai, Father Suliman (c 1966)*

Back row (left to right): *Ahmed and mini-Ebrahim.*
Middle row: *me, Ebrahim, Walla, Uncle Mohammed, micro-Ebrahim and Haji Gani. Seated: Amina Bai, Father, Grandfather Essa, Uncle Ahmed, Grandmother Heerbai.*
Front row: *Khadija, Rafique, Faizal, Saira (c. 1965)*

We moved on to the final citadel where the garbage drums are kept for collection by the City Municipality. They were housed in a dark passage that led to the residential flats above our shop. The passage had not had working lights since the Second World War was declared, some twenty three years earlier. We thought of it as a type of war memorial.

We went through six large metal trash cans.

Still no rings.

Picture Halima in her sari, Mother with her blue floral dress, my brother and Father in complete-suits-and-ties, all going through the bins, one at a time. Father sees me hesitating and barks, "What are you waiting for? Go get that bin!"

I was too scared to tell him that on the wall behind the drums lay a hive of teeming, deviously professional American, flying cockroaches. These bastards were at least 2cm larger than their 6cm cousins.

They just whizzed around, from wall to wall, above our heads and between our frames. My insensitive family couldn't be less bothered by such trivialities. They had gone to watch a film, dressed to kill, now they were purportedly prepared to die.

While all this drama was playing out, trust Mr. Sagra and his Gujarati wife – who ran a well-established grocery store next to our imitation-jewellery shop – to return home at this ungodly hour. In spite of the darkness they recognised my family immediately, and tried to walk past us and up the staircase, all while trying to keep a straight face. All Indian buildings in town had mandatory narrow passages that permitted only one-lane traffic. So they squeezed past, all the while pretending that we were not there.

*Uncle Ismail could
have been a film star
(c. 1958)*

*Amina Bai, me and
Grandmother Heerbai
(c. 1965)*

From left: Uncle Ismail, Father, Uncle Mahomed Jakaria Suleman, Haji Gani, Grandfather Essa, Walla, me and Uncle Ahmed

(c. 1964)

As soon as they were clear of the bin area, the pair of Bunyas began to breathe once more. Mr. Sagra, ever polite, turned for the last time, placed his palms together and greeted Father with 'Namaste'.

As they scuttled past, Mr Sagra muttered to his wife.

I look up, engulfed by the stink and watch the subtitles present themselves.

"See, I told you a dozen times. Everybody is going through a financial crisis nowadays. Take it easy. Don't overspend or we will also end up scavenging like them."

UDAN KHOTALA

I had five paternal uncles, four in South Africa and one in India. For some reason, each uncle had a son named Ebrahim. What a stupid idea.

It made me feel like a sausage from a boerewors factory. We decided that a prefix should be attached to each cousin's name. For instance, my uncle Ismail's son was called Mini-Ebrahim. My uncle Mohammed named his daughter Saira, but his son became known as 'micro-Ebrahim'.

Mini-Ebrahim, my brother Ahmed and I were as thick as thieves. Despite a five-year age gap between mini-Eb and I, we were inseparable. Mini-Eb lived in Prince Edward Street, but hung out with us in Albert Street on most days.

We did everything together. We watched films, wrote scripts for films that would never be shot, played soccer and carrom board, and exchanged stories and family gossip. We even almost burnt down adjacent fuel garages together.

Nothing would come between us. All for one and one for all, and all that.

Until a certain Baboo Khalek moved into Mini-Eb's neighborhood.

Baboo very swiftly took over my cousin's mind with religious dogma.

For instance, if I phoned him on a Friday night and reminded him, "EB, be here at 7:30, right? Kick off is at 8 sharp".

He would reply, "I will have to ask Baboo. I will come if he does!"

Or if I said, "Hey EB, you must come early. You will be selected on my side, as usual."

He would reply, "Yes. And Baboo, too!"

Fuck Baboo, I always thought. But it got worse.

When they did come to play, Mini-EB would only pass the ball to Baboo, even if the latter was completely out of position. It became so ridiculous that he actually stopped passing to me.

This nonsense began to extend to other areas of our lives.

It was always "Baboo this" and "Baboo this".

Ahmed and I quickly coined the phrase to describe Mini-Ebrahim's new obsession: "Godly action".

Whereas Baboo served only one God, Mini-Eb answered only to his own god, Baboo.

Ahmed and I began to pray for an opportunity to show Mini-Eb up, to make him look a little stupid.

Around 1959, my uncle Ismail – who was really passionate about American cars – decided to order a brand new Chevrolet Impala from the USA.

Mini-Eb proudly broke the news to us, as he showed us a colourful brochure with an illustration of the Blue Bel Air gliding through the clouds.

"We are getting a new Chevrolet Impala from Chicago. Totally full-house. Totally imported from American General Motors. Green, white and blue. This machine can fly, I hear!"

Poor Father (despite his rings) could not afford to buy even a blue and green bicycle for himself. So we were naturally very jealous but congratulated him anyway.

"Wow! That's something Eb! Of course it will fly through highways. Six cylinder or is it a V8? A guzzler, eh?"

And Mini-EB suddenly looked at us most seriously. "No, this machine can actually fly. I mean like a plane. Through the sky. Take off. Land. Anywhere."

Ahmed, pretending to be innocent and naïve, exclaimed, "Will it land on Baboo-and-them's roof garden?"

Mini-EB sensed he was being teased and sulkily replied, "Don't believe me, then! It's absolutely true. I tell you!"

I felt really sorry for him. Despite his growing distance from us, he was still my cousin after all. I held his hand in mine and, like a big brother, tried to gently knock some sense into him. Ahmed looked on, smiling away silently.

"Now, EB, look here. Planes fly, right? Cars normally stay on the ground, right? 'Flying' is only an expression for fast, powerful vehicles and birds, ok? Your father is merely describing its potential to kick ass on the road. Don't take it literally."

I forgot I was talking to an eight year old devotee, who was now growing emotional.

Half-sobbing, he exclaimed, "My father's name is Hajibha. And Hajibha never lies. He says it will fly.

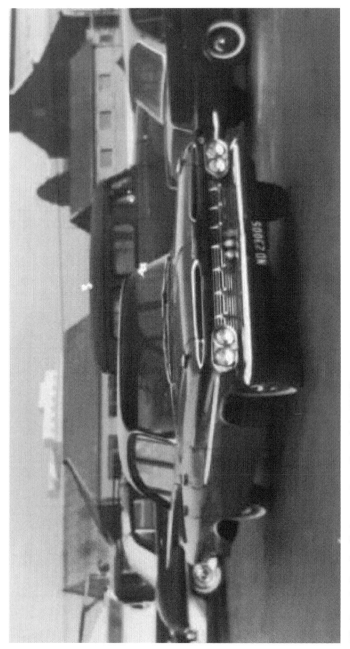

The Impala flew in all the way from Detroit (c. 1959)

It's arriving next week. Flying all the way from Detroit. You will see!"

And next week came.

The amazing, shiny blue and green Impala arrived. Talk of the town. It was so huge it took up half of Prince Edward Street.

It had 8 powerful cylinders! Jesus, Holy Christ! Tail lights and a wingspan wider than the arse of a modern Boeing 707. Wheels bigger than earthmovers used at Harry Oppenheimer's mines. Leather bench seats to seat 10 adults. Rear seats for a hundred camels. Yes! The dicky was bigger than the luggage hold of the SS Karanja!

But Hajibha, *did it fly*?

4

ANDHERI

*I had a strange dream just after passing matric in 1964.
The Mayville house was floating away, like Dorothy's in
the Wizard of Oz. Caught in a twister, it finally disappeared. Then came a flood of Biblical proportions.*

*The bay at Victoria Embankment overflowed, burst its
banks, crawled swiftly up Broad Street, entered Grey Street
and drowned Ajmeri Arcade in a matter of seconds.*

*Next, came an earthquake that shattered the Anjuman
Islam School into unholy fragments.*

*Last to vanish into dark matter was the Roman-inspired
edifice of Sastri College in Winterton Walk.*

*The nightmare however did not end with the destruction
of the monuments.*

*My best friends, Mohan and them, disappeared into the
darkness, carrying with them all our childhood memories of
fun and friendship.*

*I had seldom given much importance to my extended
family, with the exception of my uncle Ismail, who was
always my film hero, and his son Mini-Ebrahim, who had
signed a death pact with Ahmed and me.*

*Now, all my uncles, aunts, my grandfather, my grand-
mother, sisters, brothers, cousins – became vanishing
points. I had lost out badly. I never did grab the few opportunities of getting to know them a little better.*

Now, they too, had evaporated. I wake up.

I wipe the moisture from my eyes and find myself battling to keep the outline of Durban Harbour and the Bluff in focus, before they too lose their way over the edge of the earth.

I am left floating on the SS Kampala on my way to Bombay.

It's June 1965 and all the events following my matric exam in December 1964 come flashing back.

Father was in India on business, and wrote to me suggesting that I get enrolled at the University College at Salisbury Island, for a Bachelor of Science degree.

"Give it a try, and if you don't like it, I will organise admission for you in India."

I register for the 'Suicide Four' (Physics, Chemistry, Math and applied Math) and commuted by a dinky and noisy ferry daily across the Durban Bay to "try" and make it work. I battled. The sports coat and tie left me sweating. The racism left me confused. I couldn't get to grips with the courses either. I panicked and wrote to Father and asked him to intervene.

I don't know why I did. I didn't want to go to India either.

For a seventeen-and-a-half year old boy who had hardly ventured past Clairwood to now contemplate studying in another country was ridiculous.

But Father replied immediately.

"Done! Escape from that Island University and start learning some Hindi. You leave for Bombay in June!"

WATAN SE DOOR

Mr A.N Naidoo was my teacher way back in Anjuman Islam School in Standard Five.

I remember a lesson called 'A voyage to Southampton' that gave us a detailed geographical account of the British Isles.

Day after day, we visited new places through his narrations. We could taste the sweat of the coal miners of Newcastle or the Cotton Mills factory workers of Lancashire and Birmingham.

We could smell the fresh blood from the beheadings at the Tower of London.

I open my eyes. *Still trapped on the SS Kampala.*

My neck is stiff. My back is sore.

The inflatable mattress I purchased from the British India Shipping agents, Shaik Himed and Sons on Pine Street, to use on the iron-bunk of this 3rd class deck, had sprung a leak. It had just been a day of travel.

I think about home again.

Before we left, Father had thrown a party at the Ocean Terminal Restaurant in Durban, where my newlywed brother Yusuf and I were both honoured.

There was a variety of speeches by our close friends, relatives and some prominent members of the community.

All of them were great speakers but I became the talk of the town with my speech. For all the wrong reasons.

I had written the salient points on my hands but was so nervous that my sweat caused the words to smudge and I made a jackass of myself.

Before leaving the shores of Durban, I called a meeting with my friends. They would be allowed to continue with the soccer and the carrom board tournaments in my absence, I told them.

I would not be long. Only four years. Everything would be the same. Don't be sad. Smile, I thought.

Walla appeared in charge. He had moved on from being my mentor, leader and slave-driver from the Mayville-Grey Street days.

He was now married and distracted by this new attraction in his life.

Ahmed, my kid brother, was in his own world as usual. Him and I were always together; fighting or having fun. I used to take him everywhere with me, whether he liked it or not. I peered at him and wondered whether there would be a kid brother waiting for me when I returned.

I found myself revealing my innermost secrets to him at the last moment.

"Ahmed, you will find my treasured batch of secret comics, and my petite spy camera below my last drawer. Please help yourself to them all!"

And the little bastard replied: "Don't worry. I already did!"

My sisters Hawa and Halima were also beside themselves at my decision to go.

They had no recourse but to seek soulful, spiritual solace from my most pious maternal uncle, Abdul Gani Suleman, who was in charge of the Badsha Peer Shrine at Brook Street. But nothing interceded on their behalf.

Just twenty more days to reach Bombay.

Fajr azaan is loud and clear.

It was the familiar voice of my very good friend, Abdul Sattar Ganie, summoning the lazy-likes-of-me to pray.

I was not used to regular prayers, but there was no arguing with Sattar.

"We need all the help we can get," was his stellar argument.

After breakfast in a noisy congested cubicle, located next to the engine-room in the belly of this massive ship, we would go upstairs and breathe some fresh air on the deck.

No land was visible anywhere around us. The ship cut through the clear blue water, churning up a lather of white foam as it sped towards the first port of call, Lourenço Marques.

I decided to walk alone to the rearmost end of the ship and sat there. Deep in thought, I asked myself questions that no one had ever asked before, obviously.

Why does one need to study? What is the point of life? Why does one need to work? Why do people leave their homes and travel to study? Why?!

I sensed that Sattar has just joined me. He put his hands on my hunched shoulders. "Essabhai, don't worry. We will see this through together. We will be okay."

He took me back to the main deck, but even with his dark glasses on, I knew that he was crying too.

MADAM X

Father, as liberal as he was, had given me clear instructions not to disembark at any of the African ports along the way.

Most of these countries were just getting rid of the French, English or Belgian colonial brutes and independence did mean bursts of democracy and anarchy. So I was to stay-on-board.

*My sisters Halima
and Hawabai (seated)
(c. 1956)*

*My uncle, Maasa, my
maternal aunt, Maasi,
and their daughters
Farida and Amina
(seated) (c. 1958)*

At Dar es Salaam in Tanzania, most of my friends grabbed the chance of going ashore to stretch their legs. I was standing on the ship-end of the gangplank, minding my own business and regretting not having joined my friends, when a drunk Malay woman appeared out of one of the sheds on the harbour, and climbed the gangplank on her way back to the ship. She must have been about forty five, thin, tall and haggard. A face plastered in makeup and red lipstick.

A fellow passenger, and a real troublemaker, she approached me shouting, "Hey, you! Where is the guard on duty?" I figured that she had probably forgotten to get a shore pass when she had disembarked.

I decided to have some fun at her expense.

"Madam, you are in serious trouble. They won't allow you back on board. You better hide."

She heard me and went on to trip on the plank in a panic. She gathered herself, looked back at me, and realised that she had been duped.

"You got a big fucking mouth, sonny! Playing games with me, eh?" she said, before giving me a tight slap across the face.

Stunned, I slapped her right back.

Realising what I had done, I turned and ran. I ventured down some stairs below the deck into a set of male toilets. I locked myself in one. I would be safe here in this smelly cubicle, I thought. No female would dare enter male toilets. Soon enough I heard her voice as she entered the corridor and out through another set of stairs.

After what seemed like an eternity, I decided to face the music. I got up and left the fourth grade hiding place and made my way to my third class cabin. It was close to midnight now, she must have eased her search for me.

And there she was, standing next to my bunk waiting for me to return.

I turned and ran again. This time, straight to the jail on board. I figured I'd be safest there.

"Namaste Saab," I greeted the uniformed, turbaned officer sitting at a wooden table with a large register and rubber stamp at his fingertips

With nothing on me to offer, I promised him a packet of Lemon Creams the next day if he allowed me to spend the night in jail. He wanted two packets. We struck a deal and I stayed in the cell.

Next morning, he kicked me out and told me to bring the biscuits.

I still had to face that mad lady and finally plucked up some courage to meet with the consequences.

I found her having breakfast with her husband on the deck.

"Good morning, good morning. Lovely morning," I said, approaching her.

The lady smiled at me. The man greeted me.

"Nice day, nice day!" she says.

"Goolam, this is the respectable student that I was speaking to you about just now. He helped me to get on board last night when I wasn't well. Come, young man, join us for breakfast."

BOMBAY

On the night before we were due to reach Bombay, my best friend Abdul Sattar had an important meeting with me. He came across strongly: "Essabhai, we must stick together. Tomorrow is our big trial. Indian

Customs have a custom of going for the jugular of poor passengers. You don't have any luxury items with you, only because your dad – and not you – was smart. You will have to carry my Philips radio for me. Don't worry, I will be with you all the time!"

I was caught unawares but still protested, "Wait a minute, Ganie. I have this Rolleicord camera that I am carrying for my Father's best friend in Bhoiwada. And what about Goolam Omar's trunk that I am also carrying. I don't know what is in it. And they didn't give me a key."

But my protests fell on deaf ears.

Five minutes after we disembarked at 6am at Ballard Docks, C Shed, Sattar, all my friends, my enemies, even that mad woman, every one of them just disappeared.

I had a migraine even before hauling my heavy bags and trunks to customs all by myself. I had heard of these dangerous expensive coolies in red shirts and stayed clear of them.

The single cup of sweet tea I had on the ship was hours ago. I had been warned by Father to test the waters before drinking Indian water, to be wary of Indian food, Indian toilets, even Indian girls.I was told to drink only genuine American Coca-Cola, bottled in Vile Parle, and genuine South African Bakers Lemon Creams baked at Brickhill Road in Durban.

I become a little frantic.

Where was Ganie? How come his customs had been cleared so soon? Why had he not come to look for me? Where were the other South African students? And where was Goolam Omar? The arrangement back in South Africa was that he would use his influence to clear his trunk as well as all my luggage.

His father had boasted that his son had connections everywhere. But he was nowhere to be found.

Indian customs charged me the earth for other people's labachas. Ganie's Akashwani radio, Father's friend's Rolleicord camera and Goolam Omar's mysterious chest. Fortunately I had just enough rupees on me to pay the duty.

I was certain that the next stage would be easy. Find a cab, make my way to Andheri, enroll at Bhavan's College, start studying to become an engineer, get a job and get married. All in a day's work.

But it didn't take me long to realise that all the signs were in Hindi and I couldn't locate the exit. When I did finally get out, I came face to face with the monsoon. It lashed down like an endless waterfall.

We had docked at 6am. It was now 6pm and almost dark. All I knew was that I headed to a place called Andheri which I later found out means darkness. Not very consoling.

My mind raced back to the time when Father had given me a choice.

"You can become either an engineer, or come join me in the shop," he said.

Now that I was here, it was a little too late to change my mind.

I am grateful to have run into a chap named Mohamed Sharif, a returning second-year (inter-science) student, also heading for Andheri.

He sorted the luggage, and the fare for our taxi to the western suburb I was going to call home.

The taxi ride to Andheri along the central arterial, rain-lashed and formidably dark Mohammed Ali Road was surreal. My eyes filled with dread as

I watched the driver try to make sense of the dark, flooded streets. I hadn't eaten for close to 12 hours. I was also thirsty. The noisy swishing of sub-standard wiper blades on the rough, sandblasted windscreen was drowned by the continuous, deafening sound of hooting of a million horns. The black and yellow Ambassador dodged pedestrians, tiffin-carriers, other taxis, buses, cows, and horse-drawn Victorias as it splashed its path ahead. Crows and humans competed for the floating garbage on the side of the road.

HAMARA SANSAR

My hostel was located at the intersection of Dadabhai Naoroji and Versova Roads in Bombay. It was a double storey building with two and three bedroom apartments. It seemed like the demand for residential space in Andheri – especially in a district close to the squalid, dirty, poor, fishing village of Versova – was low, so the college easily rented the complete building and let it out to foreign students. It carried the well-worn cliché: 'A home away from home'. But there was simply no privacy.

Whereas other hostels had one common room for recreation, this national hostel, as it was called, had a number of common rooms. This meant that the room I was sharing with three others was a common corridor to the other students' rooms.

I shared a room with Yusuf Saloojee from Fordsburg, Abdul Sattar Ganie from Tongaat, and Narendra Patel from Zanzibar.

Yusuf Saloojee, also called Tjommie by all his close friends, was a serious and focused student. He never

*Roommates at Bhavan's College: **(Back row from left)** Abdul Sattar Gani, me, Yusuf Saloojee. **(Front row)** Narendra 'Zanzi' Patel and Sulaiman Kadwa*

forgot his umbrella, was forever boasting about the Bombay branch of the underground African National Congress (ANC), and the democracy-to-come-one-day-to-South Africa. He refused to stop smoking in our room.

Abdul Sattar Ganie, my classmate since Standard Seven at Sastri College always topped the class. He was brilliant at Mathematics and very skillful on the soccer field. Amazingly, he could write with both hands and kick equally strongly with either foot, so he became a natural choice for the left-wing position at school, college and club level.

Narendra Patel – also known as 'Zanzi' because he was from Zanzibar – was a bit of an enigma. He seldom attended lectures and was always short of cash because of the situation back home.

On my voyage from Durban on the SS Kampala, I had seen bullet holes on the palace walls along the shore of Zanzibar, where Arab Sultans had just been deposed by the Revolution in 1964. The Revolution had ended 200 years of Arab control of Zanzibar. In the chaos that followed, there was a complete embargo on all foreign exchange exiting Tanzania, leaving 'Zanzi' in a bit of a fix.

Most of his time was spent seeking out travelers that had just returned from his home country carrying with them smuggled cloth bags of cloves from his father's farm. This spice grew in abundance in Zanzibar and was in great demand in India. The contraband cloves helped him survive. But for how long?

BHAWANI JUNCTION

The lectures at Bhavan's College were a breeze for the BA students. We, who were cursed to do BSc, died every day. Sometimes twice a day. Fear, misery and depression often brought out some third grade poetry:

"Friday night is my delight,
Saturday morning till 12 I am snoring.
But Sunday night gives me a fright,
There's pracs on Monday morning"

Out of the four major subjects: physics, chemistry, mathematics, and biology, I excelled only in Additional English which counted for little.

Trust me to take an interest in the irrelevant.

Could I be blamed? I did not study Physical Science at high school because some smart arse, Ramesh Jethalal, persuaded us to petition for our Physical Science teacher to be replaced due to the high failure rate in his class the previous year. Incredibly, the petition worked; he was instantly transferred to M.L. Sultan Technical College whilst our replacement never arrived.

This forced us to change courses. I dropped Physical Science and took on commercial subjects instead. This is probably why most Gujarati boys went into business with their fathers instead of achieving their true destiny as rocket scientists.

But back to Bhavans College.

Our Physics teacher was a Maharashtrian with a bad case of red lips; the result of a daily obsession with betel leaf and betel nut with some Indian hemp, which he chewed enroute to the first year lecture hall. His blood red lips, together with his English in a thick Maratha accent, made him impossible to understand.

Then there was this short, stockily-built, moustached Mathematics lecturer from Kerala. He tried to teach us the universal language of math using the Queen's English but in an impossible-to-understand accent. It would have been easier if he just spoke to us in German.

NADI KINARE

Washing my own clothes was time consuming and a distraction from studying. Worse still, the other seven students living on the floor were threatening to murder me as I regularly monopolized the single bathroom. I finally succumbed to the private laundry service like everybody else. It was easy. The dhobi would arrive at 6am to pick up the laundry and return it the next day. The cost was minimal, or so I thought.

After a few weeks of smiling because I was now able to explore the suburbs of Bombay on the weekends, I soon noticed that my shirts were returning torn and my blue jeans were fading faster than a bunch of flowers. The dhobi's explanation was totally unacceptable.

"Saab, these clothes of yours are imported from South Africa and they are not of the same quality as the local stuff," he said.

The punk!

So I took Bus no. 252 to Amboli village to see for myself what the hell was going on.

I had been told that the laundrymen used the river that ran through this village, past the Filmalaya Studios, owned by the famous Mukherjee family.

But there was no river.

It was actually an open gutter that transported the sewerage from the numerous shacks in this village. My clothes were being 'washed' in a dark, black pig-swell full of muck.

And to think that the petite Sadhana was shooting away in the film *Love-in-Simla*, or some such musical hit with Joy Mukherjee in the studios next door. They were obviously great professionals considering they were shooting such love stories amid such a shit-stink.

Hiding behind a tree, I watched how the dhobi and his troop 'washed' clothes. Numerous garments were tightly rolled together into a rope and they struck a rough washing stone, brutally and repeatedly, as if beating a demon out of the clothes.

When I could not bear to endure any more of the pain felt by my clothes, I ran up to him and demanded an explanation.

Instead of apologising, he swore at me in Hindi.

"This is the only fucking way to get the dirt out. We all do it! Do you want your twenty five annas back?"

That was enough. I returned to hand-washing my own clothes, warding off death-threats from friends for holding the bathroom, and resigned to explore the suburbs of this magical city in my next life. Inshallah.

ROTI

Man cannot survive by studies alone. I needed to eat but when you have been warned about the high frequency of diarrhoea, dysentery, typhoid and cholera – from even the five star hotels across the city – it was hard to trust the food and water I found on campus.

Most of my friends dined at Rajkumar's Lounge, a local canteen on Bhavan's campus. I once ordered some curried baked beans and buttered bread, but gave up and walked out when I could not distinguish between the beans and the flies.

Inmates at the hostel tried their unwashed hands at cooking their own food using a low-pressure kerosene stove. We pooled our resources. Some chopped onions and tomatoes, others peeled potatoes, others washed the dishes. Some did the actual cooking. And some, well, came by just to eat. The plan eventually flopped because the hanger-ons increased and there were just too many people to feed. The yellow-blue flame of the paraffin cooker had to be extinguished.

COLLEGE STORY

There is a timeless saying in Urdu:

"Pareh Angrezi Beche Thel
Yeh Dekho Kismat Ka Khel…"

"Studied for a profession but dropped out to sell
cheap, contaminated cooking oil, to poverty-stricken
informal settlements…"

I had left the shores of sunny South Africa and embraced the muddy shores of Bombay with just one intention – to become an engineer. Not only did I not know how to spell the word but I had no idea what it meant. So, meanwhile, I kept busy by ogling all the local girls. The prettiest ones were mostly in the Arts and Social Studies departments. There was one particular firebrand who always wore a colourful cotton salwar kameez. Her name was Kanchan.

She was a tall and beautiful woman with a roundish face; a fair complexion with a beauty spot just like Helen from the movies. She looked like such a nice Muslim girl, always wearing a scarf on her head. I was a nice Muslim boy. I was decent and good looking. Surely she would be my heroine. She would never even think of warding me off.

Until a friend warned me, "She is a Sikh, not a Muslim. Her parents will roast you and then drown her with shame in the first well they find in Amritsar!"

When I tried to find out more, a Hindu friend urged me to forget the whole thing. He refused to indulge any further. I slowly began to understand that it might have had something to do with the bad blood between Sikh, Hindu and Muslim communities from the time of partition. It was 1965 so it was all still fresh. Those of 'faint heart never won a fair maiden' but I was a sheep in sheep's clothing and instantly forgot about Kanchan forever.

But my time spent around the Arts and Social Studies Department did not go to waste.

One day while making a scene in the department – I may have been reciting poetry to an amused audience – I was approached by the head of the English department. Miss Cynthia Pais, an Anglo-Indian woman, addressed me formally.

"Mr Essa, have you heard of the *Wall Paper*?"

Of course I knew about the *Wall Paper* magazine that was published on the campus notice board. I knew of its glorious past. It published everything from news to original poetry, short stories and even illustrations sent in by the college fraternity.

But the quality of the magazine had faded of late. It was rarely updated. Nobody seemed interested in it any more. I knew all of this already but here she was asking me to revive it.

I resisted, explaining that I was struggling with my core subjects of science and mathematics, was way behind with my practical reports, had piles of washing to do since my discovery of the gutter in Amboli, and was critically uncertain about where my next meal, free-of-flies, was coming from.

"Ma'am, get a local student to do this, please. Somebody from the Arts Department? This is really out of my league."

Her smiling reply was, "I cannot believe your modesty. You will really have very little to do. Just call for contributions and you will receive so many that your only problem will be to decide which ones to reject. Also, many students will be willing to assist to put them up on the notice board. It's a real pushover. You will see."

I came. I saw. I was pushed over.

Miss Pais – bless her dyed, golden-brown, neat, short hair and her pious, Christian, Anglo-Indian soul – turned out to be a real con-artist. Nobody helped. Nobody contributed. It became totally my baby. I became poet, cartoonist, writer, news collector and editor all by my poor self. I even resorted to

A sample of one of the numerous cartoons drawn for The Wallpaper
(c. 1967)

using fictitious names for my articles to make the magazine look authentically diverse.

As if that was not enough, English professor and also self-elected president of the Foreign Students Union (FSU), Mr Khan, also approached me for some help. He was thin and tall and always wore a light brown suit even in the worst of Indian summers. He reminded me of Muhammad Ali Jinnah, the founder of Pakistan.

Mr Khan said he wanted me to contribute to the college magazine. He tried to sweeten his request by saying that KM Munshi, the founding president of the college, would receive a copy too.

I could not understand. Hundreds of millions of people in India but both Miss Pais and Mr Khan could only find me, a complete newcomer from a foreign land, to do their dirty work?

"Can I write about anything?" I asked with a devilish grin.

"Yes! Yes! Go ahead! You know I have just been appointed warden of the National Students' Hostel. If you ever need anything at the hostel. Let me know."

Mr Khan clearly had a lot of confidence in me. What damage could a sweet lad like me accomplish anyway?

My article was titled: *"A home away from home"* and it spoke of the shocking conditions at the hostel and how unhappy the residents were living in the overcrowded hellhole.

A local student even added to the intended mayhem by drawing a cartoon next to my comments. Mr Khan came running to my room, soon after the magazine had been published and distributed. He looked frantic.

"Ebrahim, what have you done? This is going to cost me the warden's post!"

I tried to console him, telling him that it was worth the loss to embarrass the college administration into improving the living conditions of students. I felt sorry for him.

"Mr Khan, to make it up to you, I have decided to lead the debating team at the FSU showdown between foreign students and the local students. I like the topic, 'Should India use nuclear weapons in a war with Pakistan?'".

Mr Khan composed himself. I knew he was going to forgive me. Instead he goes on to scream, "No! You will do no such thing. You are far too dangerous."

BORDER

Life became a little hectic. I faced constant harassment from Miss Pais regarding *Wall Paper* deadlines.

Then there was Mr Khan stalking me just a day after turning down my offer to lead the FSU debate. It is not like he had forgiven me. He just couldn't find anyone else to do the job. Meanwhile, the food situation had become desperate because my Lemon Cream biscuits supply had run out. My practicals were becoming practically impossible to complete. I was washing and ironing my own clothes and being overlooked even as a ball boy in the Bhavan College Soccer Tournament (just because I could not kick a ball). And it was about to get worse.

India-Pakistan skirmishes on the border in 1965 turned into a full scale war.

This disturbed me. Why have a war when I had been in this challenging country for less than six months?

I couldn't fathom physics, math or chemistry in broad daylight. How would I ever cope with handling these demons during the blackouts at night? What about my report on Ohm's law? It was already five weeks overdue and there was no way Dr GZ Shah, head of the Physics department, was going to give me another extension.

I then received an urgent telegram from Father in South Africa.

Please pack up and prepare for evacuation.

I panicked. I dodged the blackout and I rushed to Andheri Post Office to reply.

Relax Father! It's not that bad!

I was not lying. It was not that bad. It was just fucking bad!

That said, comparing it to Durban where nothing exciting ever happened besides Tommy Chetty's merry-go-round, where international soccer and cricket teams avoided us like the plague, and where I would ordinarily be selling bloody bangles at Bombay House to clumsy customers… No thank you Father! I will settle for this war instead. Unfortunately, all bad things must come to an end. The skirmishes that took place in Kashmir and on the India-Pakistan border lasted for some months before ending in early 1966.

There is an attempt at a ceasefire in Tashkent, Uzbekistan. It succeeds.

I am happy, but disappointed. I now have no alibi for performing badly in the mid-term exams. Also, no reason for the exams to be cancelled either.

As both India and Pakistan count their losses, in both economic and body bag terms, I return to my desk to complete that dismal report on Ohm's law.

MUSAFIR

Colleges are closed for the whole of October for the festival of Deepavali: the festival of lights.

It is also the season when hostel authorities kicked all the students out on to the street under the standard pretext that they are renovating and repairing the place. Nobody warned me about this, despite everybody else knowing. I had barely survived a long, drawn-out war lasting some two weeks and I now have to look for a refugee camp within twenty four hours.

All my friends had made their plans:

Rasik (from East Africa): "I am touring the south of India. Got my student-concession tickets all worked out."

Ganie (from Western Tongaat): "I am going to Porbandar, near Jamnagar, to visit my relatives."

Saloojee (from Central Fordsburg): "I am heading for Randher, near Surat, for no clear reason."

Zanzi (from somewhere between the islands of Pemba and Zanzibar): "I am in shit. I have no money left and I have failed all my exams."

I begin to panic and hurriedly rummage through a notebook used as diary, grocery list and lecture notebook, until I find a name.

Haji Abdul-Latif Ali Mohamed
General Dealer
P.O. Ghatanji
District Yeotmal
Jillo Barar

I was thrilled to discover that I have somewhere to go.

My uncle, Abdul Gany Suleman – whom we called Maasa – had given this address to me before I left South Africa. It was an address he had written down before he had left India for South Africa 35 years earlier.

Haji Mohamed is Mother's brother. But I had no idea where Jillo Barar was.

It took me days – and a trip to Mohammad Ali Road in Bombay, also known as Memon resource centre – to get a sense of where to go. A supariwala told me to go to Yeotmal, near Nagpur, in the middle of Maharashtra State.

Before I knew it, I had jumped on Howrah Mail, a second class sleeper train at Victoria Terminus in Bombay, and headed towards Yeotmal. I jumped off at Dhamangaon. Here, I saw a scrawny fellow running towards me in a white dhoti. He grabbed my bags with enthusiasm.He chewed on a betel leaf and spit red muck on the tracks.

Then I heard someone shout at him in crisp Hindi, followed by a greeting in English. There was someone behind the man in the dhoti.

"Leave that to me. It's okay. I will take care of your luggage. Hi! I am your cousin, Haroon."

I look up at a tall, handsome, healthy young man wearing a long-sleeved, white, silk shirt, grey pants and an expensive pair of leather sandals. He also has a pair of sunglasses that look like pirate Rayban wayfarers.

"Who?" I enquire.

"Haroon. My father is your mama. Your mother's brother."

5

GHATANJI

A cousin. I have no cousin beyond Chatsworth. But I find myself following him as he leads me to a bus.

"This is Dhamangaon," he says, as we enter the bus.

"We will go to Yeotmal. From there we will catch another local bus to my village, Ghatanji."

I listen intently and closely to him. A cousin in the middle of India? I cannot believe it.

How could he speak so well if he hailed from an insignificant, probably non-existent village? Why is he not barefoot, dirty, and wearing torn clothes? Why is he not unshaven, with bad breath, scratching violently at the lice in his hair? Why is he not confusing me with a mixed dialect of Memon, Urdu, Marathi and Hindi.

I am so confused.

Sensing my hunger he takes me to a tin shack selling food. There are wooden tables and benches outside. Before I can stop him he has already ordered two plates of mutton curry and four chapatis. He also requests two glasses of water. Around us, a pair of pigs go about their business, hogging in the open gutters. I remember I am in India.

"Haroon Bhai, I just remembered I had a massive breakfast on the train. Maybe I can have a cup of tea?"

I am too afraid to offer to pay for the wasted curry, fearing that he might take it as an insult. When he sees my difficulty swallowing the tea, served in a stained china cup, he frowns. But he is so smart looking. Why can't he understand?

We reach Yeotmal after a couple of hours. I am now tired, nauseous, hungry, thirsty, and anxiously preparing myself to catch the next bus to Ghatanji. I hope a clean home-bath, clean home-food, a clean home-toilet, a clean home-bed and kind homely words would comfort me.

Ten minutes after we reach Yeotmal, Haroon announces casually, "We have just missed the last bus so we will put up at my rented lodge tonight."

I rush to the toilet. No lights. No running water. No soap. Not even a toilet pan. There is, however, a hole in the ground. I remain constipated.

I settle down on to the coir-mattress, whilst Haroon takes the floor.

I am exhausted from the bizarre events of the last twenty-four hours. My first long-distance train journey in India, my first meeting with a relative outside of South Africa, all while starving and thirsty for the last twelve hours.

I decide that no mosquito, bedbug, mite, asthma, eczema, allergy nor the stench of my own unwashed body and atrocious breath, would keep me awake tonight.

I do not sleep a wink.

In the morning, I discover that the bus waiting to carry us to our final destination is a flat-bed truck with seats bolted at the back. It seems custom-made for fakirs and other ascetic souls searching for self-flagellation as a path to nirvana. The driver is also a handpicked expert in sadism; his sole purpose is to punish all who ventured on this trip. He never misses a pothole on the dirt track.

Some of us finally reached Ghatanji alive. We bury the martyrs at a longtime gravesite alongside the bus stand.

AUNTY NO.1

My maternal uncle, Haji Abdool Latif – or Mama – was a gaunt, white-bearded man of average height. He must have been around 50 years old but looked older in a kurta-pajama and skullcap.

After greeting me warmly for about a minute, he asked about my mother – his sister – whom he had not seen for over forty years.

He wanted to know everything. Haroon translated the long conversation.

"So, how is your mother?"

"She's okay, I think," I replied.

"Good! Let's eat!"

My aunt, who had a large smile and a mole under her nostrils, was a bit more thorough, asking me about each and every relative. She spoke in Memon, and the only phrase I knew at this time was "teek aye" which roughly translates to "is okay".

And so she began her interrogation: "So, how is Zulekafui?"

My reply: "Teek aye."

"And Kairoonkaki?"

"Teek aye."

And "Noorbai Masi?"

"Teek aye!"

And "Machardhiani?"

"Teek aye!"

At this last response she gave me a heavy slap on my back, taking out what little wind I had in my lungs. She laughed.

"Ha! There is no such person. It means mosquito net. You liar!" Haroon said, chuckling.

I felt so helpless as my aunt continued to rattle on about her other relatives in South Africa. This time I offered no comment.

Then came the food.

"Mehmaan jaan se pyara hota hein"

Hot mutton curry was served with options of rice or roti. A spicy side of dhall, and accompaniments of pickles and papad completed the meal. Dessert was a white, sweet rice pudding with raisins. Then tea and sweets.

God bless my Auntie.

MAMAJI

Mother's only brother, Haji Abdool Latif, was hard of hearing in one ear. So he merely ignored you if you got on the wrong side of him. Sometimes I got the impression that he pretended to be deaf in both ears, or maybe he could not remember which ear it was.

I did all the talking, very loudly. I wanted to know about my Mother as a young woman.

"What did she like doing? What were her favourite games? Did she ever try swimming in that river that flowed behind the house? Or after the monsoon? Did she ever venture far from the main house? Did she ever go for walks beyond the mountains; herding sheep, goats and cows? Did the river dry up in summer? Where were the schools that she was never allowed to go to?"

I was really disappointed at his silence, despite my talking at great length and volume at his good ear. Then Haroon reminded me that his father did not understand a word of English.

Mama used a special language to wake me for the early morning prayers. He used to first twist my ears whilst I was fast asleep, gently, so he would not disturb me too much. Then he would grunt something, and when I opened my eyes, he'd point to the ceiling with one finger while wearing a simultaneously fearful and fearsome frown. I wondered why he didn't push his sons as he pushed me to attend prayers at the mosque before sunrise.

After a refreshing jog to the river, we would return in time for breakfast. Fried eggs, roti saturated with melted clarified butter and hot, sweet tea would invariably meet us.

My uncle's business was a hardware store located at the front of the house. Everything in that shop moved at a snail's pace. For instance, a turbanned, tired and swarthy farmer would double park his bullock cart outside on the dusty street. He'd walk into the store, greet my cousins and uncle, complain about rains that had failed again that year, comment about Congress and what a mess the post-independence government had made out of the country. After muttering something about heavy bullock traffic on the village roads, he'd actually get to the point of his visit to the store.

After this first and only customer for the morning, my uncle would stretch out his hands and declare it lunch and Zohr time.

At lunch, when my aunt asked my uncle how business was coming along. He would shake his head and say that it was "busy; so busy".

*Above: My stylish cousin
Haroon from a village near
Nagpur (c. 1967)*

*Right: My mother's only brother,
my Mama, Abdul Latif. (c. 1965)*

EK GAON KI KAHANI

Everybody loves villages, farms, horses, cows and green fields. Nobody wants to get up at 4 am, and prepare for daily chores.

Everybody loves fresh milk and Jersey cows. Nobody likes walking foot-first into mud, and then stepping head-first into fresh, hot cow dung.

Everybody loves golden and evergreen trees and lush meadows spread out without the restriction of grotty, modern buildings and skyscrapers. Nobody likes open sewers, septic tanks, no-flush toilets and bottle-green arsed flies.

Before getting here, I had become a master city slicker in Bombay. In this metropolis for the feisty and the furious I jumped on fast suburban trains at Churchgate and learned how to purposely hang outside the train doors just to defy death. I had also memorised many of the Bombay Electric Supply & Transport Undertaking (B.E.S.T) bus routes, and was able to tell where they were going, despite route numbers being in Hindi or Marathi.

I knew all the shortcuts, alleys and gullies.

Imagine being able to watch Hindi films as soon as they were released at movie houses located at the doorsteps of the residences of the film stars themselves.

So what was I doing in this rustic village with a population of 10 000 people, suffering from a lack of basic creature comforts that I had become so used to in the city?

Ghatanji, like most other villages of India, boasted open gutters that emitted horribly bad odours and even worse bacteria. Light green dung from cows with diarrhea and dark brown from healthy handsome bulls, splattered all over the sandy roads and fields.

Haroon's family in Ghatanji (c. 1965)

Haroon's Mother and I (c. 1965)

Dirty, dubious drinking water from the well at the back of the house had mosquitoes to match. Armadas of bottle-green flies, not much smaller than the Russian-built GNAT air force planes used by India in their recent B-grade war with Pakistan, droned in the yard.

The toilet, a square hole in the ground surrounded by corrugated iron walls, was where human excreta was regularly removed, most often by lowly-paid-scheduled-caste-female hands. Sometimes even as one was defecating. The climate during October was upwards of 40⁰C. And the cherry on top; a bug house of a single cinema which showed the same Indian movie for weeks and weeks (Mere Sanam (1965) with Biswanjit and Asha Parekh seemed to play for forever).

But I stayed on for a complete month without a complaint. The need for material discomforts evaporated. The sincere love and affection demonstrated by all my uncle's family towards this heavenly relative from Africa, added to the aura of the village. This was the village in which my Mother had grown up. I was in awe. So much so, I felt as if this was my place of birth and belonging, as well.

BAGHBAAN

One day, while still in Ghatanji my cousin Haroon insisted that we visit an old lady whom he addressed as 'Wadima' (Big Mother).

She lived a few doors away from my uncle's house. They were middle-class, friendly, hospitable and even offered a decent meal. Eventually it was time to go. But I failed to spot an old octogenarian in our midst.

I whispered to Haroon if there had been some misunderstanding as to the purpose of our visit.

He whispered back, asking me to be patient. "Later", he said.

On our way out, just before we could reach the main exit, he asked me to follow him down a short flight of stairs that led to a stable behind the house. There, amongst cows and goats was a bed made with a wooden frame. It supported a very thin coir mattress. Seated on the bed with her very thin, bare feet hardly touching the floor was Wadima. The grand old lady herself. Wizened, hunched, very frail, virtually bald, and almost blind.

Haroon whispered that she is over eighty years of age, but she looks at least a hundred to me.

"Why is she living here?" my face asked and Haroon, as if expecting this question, answers with a well-prepared statement.

"She is the great-grandmother of this house. She prefers living like this."

"How do you know?" I persist.

Haroon replies, trying very hard to keep a straight face as he hurriedly beckons me to follow him up the stairs, out of the house, and onto the dusty, dark street outside, "Her children say so."

HUMSAFAR

In 1965, my onward journey to Dhamangaon had been booked at Victoria Terminus, Bombay. It was the starting point, so there was no difficulty in reserving a berth.

This was certainly not the position for my return trip. I only obtained an unreserved ticket on the day I decided to leave Ghatanji, to get back to Bhavan's College, in time for the start of the second semester. At

Dhamangaon, just before I clambered onto the coach, Haroon anxiously enquired once again if I would manage without a reserved seat. He looked worried as the train seemed pretty full.

"Of course I will be okay. Nothing to stress over. Had a lovely time. Regards to all. Visit me in Bombay someday. Bye!"

I was forced to say all this in a clutter of fast talk. Dhamangaon was an irrelevant, piss-arse stop to Indian Railway Administration, so trains stopped here for barely 30 seconds.

Of course I would be fine, Haroon! Especially as I did not mind standing at the very same spot for sixteen hours without food or water, unable to reach into my jeans pocket for my handkerchief, separated very quickly from my luggage. I was completely okay with being in contact with hundreds of other commuters breathing in my face continuously, unable to reach a toilet, experiencing a fever brought on by an infected fungal foot, suffering nausea, and trying hard to ignore an asthmatic wheeze in my chest. Oh yes, Haroon. I was fine.

HOSPITAL

A week after returning from Ghatanji, I was diagnosed with jaundice.

My close friends, ably led mainly by Abdul Sattar Ganie and Yusuf Saloojee, saved my life by getting me timeously admitted to J.J. Hospital, in Byculla, Bombay. But not without a twist.

After admitting me, Abdul Sattar Ganie brought me a bottle of some pale yellow liquid during visiting hours at J.J. Hospital. Weak as I was, I forced a smile and asked him politely, "What is this Ganie? Horse piss?"

Ganie: "Sugarcane juice. Homeopathically approved for Kamro."

Me: "What?!" (Very weakly)

Ganie: "Kamro is the Memon name for yellow jaundice."

Me: "Where did you get it from?"

Ganie: "A shop. A proper one. You think I got this off the road?"

Me: "Well…I am not drinking that stuff. I would rather die."

Ganie: "You will if you don't drink it, idiot! It was a proper, clean, well established, brick and cement shop Eb."

Now I was certain that Sattar was lying. Yes, it might have been a 'proper' shop. Maybe with walls of brick and cement and marble floors from Agra. I didn't care. As far as I was concerned, it wasn't clean. This was Bombay.

I did not have the strength to win this battle with Ganie, so I told him that I would have it later.

I poured it down the drain a few minutes later.

NASIHAT

During apartheid in South Africa we seldom got to see international soccer teams competing with our national team, as most of the civilized world had imposed an embargo on all cultural, trade and sports ties with the Republic. In addition, all citizens of the Western world were indoctrinated to hate Russia and Communism. Besides being forced to read George Orwell's *Animal Farm* at school, I had also seen enough Sean Connery James Bond movies to have no doubt that Russians were downright unforgivable villains and not nice people.

While I was still in hospital, I saw a full page advertisement in the *Indian Express* about an international soccer match between a team from the Soviet Union and India near Churchgate, Bombay, the following week. I jumped up in excitement. The nagging pain in my liver suddenly turned sharp, reminding me that my liver was still swollen from the Hepatitis A virus. I could not contain my excitement.

I was 19 years old; old enough to make logical, mature, intelligent decisions without consulting anybody. I walked out backwards, so nobody would make out that I was actually leaving the hospital. The nearest public call box miraculously worked the first time, and I managed to call my best friend Abdul Sattar Ganie, who I begged to "Just get me the cheapest ticket for the game!"

By another miracle, a ticket was delivered in a few days, right to my bed. I wondered why my best friend would address the letter to "spoiled brat". No matter! I was already planning my next letter to my brother, Walla, back in darkest Africa.

Guess who I saw playing football with our motherland?

Yes! Red-blooded Russians. In the flesh. The kind Sean Connery kicked around in *From Russia with Love*.

You know how we hate Russians. More than we hate Americans, who hate the British. Bloody communists. Go suck Karl Marx's arse.

And so on and so on.

I tried to think up all the exaggerated bile I could include in my letter about communism, capitalism, imperialism, apartheidism. Sadist that I was, I just wanted to make Walla and Ahmed jealous and annoyed at my opportunity.

The big Sunday arrives and the physician in charge of my ward arrives early; he has plans to take his family out to Powai Lake near Goregaon, for a picnic later.

"My, you are looking very excited today, Mr. Essa. How are you feeling?"

"One hundred percent Doc! I am taking a taxi this afternoon to watch the game near Churchgate. Back by 6pm. Organise me a day pass, please. Thank you!"

"You are not only sick in the liver but also sick in the head, my friend. You are not going anywhere."

I show him my precious ticket and point to my lips.

"Doc, read my lips. I have a ticket. I will be careful. I am going in a taxi. I will go slowly and will be careful."

"This is INDIA, young man. You can't be careful. One hard jolt to your liver and you could be a goner."

"Come on! I know how to look after myself!"

"Since you insist, I will give you something better than just a day pass. I can discharge you. Permanent discharge."

"Er..."

"Go back to bed and listen to the commentary on that radio of yours. It is far safer."

The ticket went to waste. I heard the Soviet team thrashed the Indian team. But that radio; It was the Philips radio I had carried for Abdul Sattar on the ship all those months ago.

LAGAAN

The West Indian cricket team would never be coming to tour South Africa, not under apartheid at least. I had already missed the Russian soccer match and lost the opportunity to write a tongue-wagging letter back home, so when I saw the West Indian cricket team would be in India for a test series in 1966, I knew I couldn't miss it. The first test was taking place at the Brabourne Stadium – just across the road from Churchgate Railway Station – in Bombay. I immediately made plans to see the game.

The first day of the match would be Sunday. I quickly picked up a blue airmail aerogramme and wrote to the brother that I loved most to bother.

"Dear Walla, guess what? West Indies on their way here. Gary Sobers, the works! Playing in Bombay. And I am going!"

Walla replied – not an ounce of green envy leaking through the mail – also by blue aerogramme.

"Go for it man! Buy your ticket early. Just get there. You so lucky!"

I purchased the cheapest ten-rupee ticket I could afford, weeks in advance. I packed an apple, orange, egg sandwiches, and a bottle of cold Coke into my kit bag, also a week in advance.

On the first day of the test match, I secured an Andheri-Churchgate return ticket in anticipation of a rush after the game.

The queue to get into the stadium was already overflowing onto the pavement, much to the annoyance of the regular street booksellers whose business was being affected badly. It took forever but I eventually found myself in a section of the line that was in a subway below the pavilion. To understand what transpired in the next few minutes, one has to fully appreciate that there were five million people living in Bombay in 1966.

And it appeared to me that all five million had arrived at Brabourne Stadium to watch India demolish the Windies.

Little did I know that everything else in their path would be demolished too.

It started when the queue suddenly stopped moving. It then started moving backwards. Cricket administrators might have sold a few more tickets than the available seats. Maybe a few million more.

Patrons from another entrance collided with our queue. From the sound of it, the first ball had been bowled. The test match had begun. We could not see a thing. We were all busy down here, battling to survive our own test.

My kit bag was the first casualty. Goodbye stale egg sandwiches. Somebody's fingers were in the back pocket of my jeans. Goodbye wallet, college ID and locker key. Then, my rubber beach thongs went, torn from under my toes.

My silly head was now being uprooted from its mid-on position.

My eyeballs were being squeezed out of their sockets like the bails being removed in slow motion. Simply put, I was like a maiden being run over by a roller.

I had been lazy to learn Hindi up to this point, but decided it was time to make an effort. It seemed as if my life depended on it. I strung together enough words to scream out that I was a foreigner who needed to breathe. I wanted out. I wanted to leave. I don't know what happened next but somebody obviously heard me.

I was picked up and carried like a corpse by the crowd and taken to exit. I ended up on the pavement. My shirt torn in different places, my jeans tangled and stretched. I sat on the floor next to puddles of betel nut spit.

Nobody gave me even a second look. This was Bombay, after all.

As I sat on the floor I searched frantically for my train ticket. I found it! In my back pocket! There is a God after all! I could go home to my shitty studies. What a great idea! Fuck the cricket. Fuck Sobers. Fuck the Indians.

In my next letter to Walla, I wrote: "I may attend the All-India-hopscotch-championship-for-physically-challenged-Tibetan-refugees, next month. Think I should take a chance?

EK ARMAAN MERA

As soon as the first year science exams were over, Father arrived unannounced from South Africa, and called me to the Sea Face Hotel in Churchgate.

He wanted to go on a holiday around northern India with me. He asked me to plan the trip.

I was thrilled. Straightaway, I began to collect maps, check out routes, compare rates at different hotels, and enquire about the most interesting places to visit in the famous golden triangle of Delhi, Agra and Jaipur. I had never been anywhere alone with Father before. He had always been busy; battling to make ends meet. Now I was about to have him all to myself.

This was my big opportunity to really try and understand this man!

Up to this point, I saw him as somebody to be really afraid of.

Fearless, frustrated, ill-tempered, anxious, often-introverted, asthmatic, and constantly harassed by hayfever. He knew everything worth knowing; all the laws, all the loopholes. A legend, despite failing to pull off that gold smuggling epic.

I could just picture this vacation. A 19-year-old son, a 56-year-old father. Wow! We would really paint the Great Fort of Delhi red; pass some memorable time at Jantar Mantar; watch the Son-et-Lumiere Show wide-eyed from the cheap seats as crackling speakers to recount India's glorious and sometimes inglorious history from the Mughal period, through the British Raj and finally to independence.

We'd climb to the highest floor of the Qutub Minar, even if it means bribing the attendant; investigate the secret tunnels at Fatehpur-Sikri through which legendary Anarkali was allowed to escape from the glances of Dilip Kumar; sit around the Anup Talao and contemplate how the originator of classic musical ragas, Tansen, was able to light candles through his music alone; hire our own tanga and gallop around the Pink Palace in Jaipur, by beating the life out of those poor, half-starved, doubly overworked Indian horses; perform Friday prayers at Shah Jahan's Jama Masjid; and wade through the crowded markets of Chandni Chowk without buying a thing.

By 8am on Monday morning, March 25 1966, everything was planned. I just needed a nod from Father, who was now expected back from Gujarat on the

Flying Rani train at about 10am, and we would be on our way to a dream come true.

Half an hour later, he walked straight into the breakfast hall of the hotel, but was not alone. His sister and her husband, Aunty Mariam and Uncle Dawood, were by his side.

They had arrived unexpectedly from South Africa and were also on holiday. He had to discuss something urgently with my uncle, and so excused himself and promised to return for breakfast in ten minutes. "Order extra tea and some toast".

As soon as Father and uncle were out of sight, my aunt hugged me, most uncharacteristically, then fired away, "Ebrahim, your father told us about the tour you are planning to Delhi and Agra. Your uncle and me will be coming too. We want to go to Ajmer to see the shrine. I know, I know, Ajmer was not part of your itinerary. Include it and delete Jaipur. I know everything about those holy shrines, that we will give total preference to. Also omit all those silly historical places your father mentioned. The Mughals were unholy, unIslamic barbarians. Very overrated. I have convinced your dad that you will not act childish and drag us into any dirty, smelly, urine-stinking, secret tunnels in those horrible forts, either. Delete forts and ruins. Grow up, dear nephew. Anarkali and Tansen – all fiction. I have already convinced your father about my plans for you on this tour. It's brilliant. You will see!"

Of course my aunt actually never said any of this. But I knew her and suddenly lost all interest in the trip.

Me "bored" in Ajmer (c. 1966).

BAAP RE BAAP

Father was born in Jodiya, Gujarat, on Christmas Day in 1910.

They were not well off. Nobody was in those days. Conditions at their house, whether the food or the living arrangements, were horrible. The toilet, for instance. Well, there was no such thing. There was an open-air enclosure outside the house where they would take a brass container, choose a spot, squat, and do their thing. It was, I suspect, the main reason my father emigrated to South Africa.

Let us move now to our 1966 tour de force.

Father knew that I had become despondent since my uncle and aunt decided to join us. He reassured me that nobody would be allowed to change any of my plans and that he would send them ahead to a town called Karanja, near Nagpur, to visit some Bibi Sahab Dargah. Once they were done with the shrines, we would meet up with them in Nagpur later and do the tour together, exactly as planned.

"Father, since we have those extra days to ourselves, I would like to take you to Ghatanji."

"Why do we need to go there? It's not on the main route."

"Yes. I know. But my mama! His family. Mother was born there, you know?"

"Don't I know? I got married there. Too many flies.

"Nah. Not that bad, actually. We will manage."

"Really! So how did you manage to catch jaundice last time you were there?"

"We're not sure it came from there. Anyway, I am fine now."

"And the toilet? The toilet at your mama's house?"

Father (left) and Mama with his family in Ghatanji (c. 1966)

Auntie Mariam and Uncle Dawood with Father (right) at Humayan's Tomb, Delhi (c. 1966)

"Pa, it is a tin hut. Just block your nose. It is only for four days!"

"Okay. But I don't like it at all…"

It was Father's first trip to Ghatanji in about forty years. Needless to say they went crazy when they saw him. They couldn't stop thanking me for bringing him.

After we left the village and boarded the train for Nagpur, I asked Father how he had found the village. Was it as bad as he thought it would be? Father said it was okay, besides avoiding the toilet for four complete days.

ANARKALI

My uncle and aunt finally struck a working compromise with Father and I. We would not accompany them to the shrines but they would accompany me to the forts.

Almost every place of interest we visited carried an element of intrigue or mystery. For instance, around the Qutub Minar there were clear signs of idols, belonging to ancient temples that had their eyes gouged out and the area converted into a mosque.

Nobody was allowed to climb to the highest levels of the minaret anymore. Drama writers, otherwise known as tour guides, insisted the reason was to prevent moonstruck lovers from committing suicide. Anyone who wanted to do that now would have to make it to the afterlife from the lower levels.

HOWRAH BRIDGE

Medical seats at university had always been difficult to come by. The same can be said of engineering. In India, two engineering seats were reserved for South African students, due to the Indian government's commitment to assist victims of apartheid, as well as to continue cultural ties with the Indian diaspora. In 1966, I was fortunate enough to have been offered a seat. Apparently my application had been too exceptional to turn down. It was apparently also the only application they had received that year.

Jairam, a close friend of mine from Kenya, was also a person of Indian origin, and was nominated for such a seat as well. Coincidentally, both of us had been selected to attend the Howrah Government College of Engineering in the city of Howrah; a mere 15km from Calcutta.

Everybody was thrilled except Father, who was still in Bombay after our exciting tour of Northern India.

"Howrah is on the other side of the subcontinent. It will not be easy to visit you from South Africa. Also, the Bengali people are not very friendly."

I could not understand. This was Bengal. The land of Rabindranath Tagore, Saratchandra Chatterjee and Satyajit Ray.

Three days later we were there.

Howrah and Calcutta are separated by the Hooghly River which flows into the Bay of Bengal. Linking the two cities is a massive iron structure called Howrah Bridge. A year earlier the government of India renamed it Rabindra Seth after Tagore, but no one ever called it that.

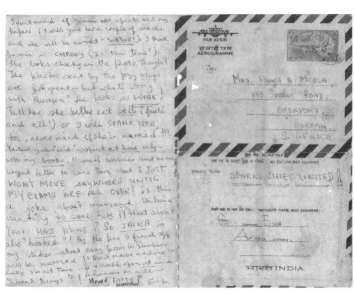

Letter to Hawabai (c. March 1967)

Designed and constructed by the British, this incredible engineering feat carried thousands and thousands of cycle-rickshaws, horse-driven victorias, taxis, cyclists, cows, goats and pedestrians, each day and night.

The noisy, lively, resounding reverberation around this City of Joy was exciting and deafening, but also quite intimidating. Even if Bombay was a lot more congested, I had grown to love its insatiable buzz. Calcutta just didn't do it for me.

The man at the Engineering College registration desk, told me there were no more seats left in the electrical engineering course. If I wanted to study at the college, I would have to do telecommunications.

I protested, showing him the letter from India's Ministry of External Affairs which promised me a seat in electric engineering. But I was told to make up my mind by the morning. They had hundreds of takers for the telecommunications seat, too.

Before I made up my mind, I was curious about my friend Jairam, who had left Bombay about a week before me, to take up his mechanical engineering seat. The clerk, most impatiently waiting for me to depart, informed that though Jairam had been granted admission into mechanical engineering, he had turned it down and disappeared.

On returning to Bombay, I confronted Jairam who had his own tale to tell.

"Those Bengali bastards at the hostel! They made me sleep in the open fields for nights on end!"

"So what's so bad about that? It was steamy hot there."

"They went through all my belongings."

"So?"

"I was told that we had no business coming back to India. They were just horrible."

And on and on, Jairam carried on. I heard him out. Felt sorry for him. Felt sorrier for myself but finally rushed to Seaface Hotel to tell Father what I had understood from the entire episode.

"I know why Bengal has been blessed with such wonderful authors and philosophers. Same reason why Islam arrived in Arabia first. Those Bengali idiots really needed them the most."

MAUSAM

Getting booted out of Bengal was the cherry on top of all the problems I had encountered since I landed here twelve months ago. Or so I thought.

In Bombay the monsoon had not come and a spectacular drought was in motion.

Dark clouds continued. But high command did not authorise rain.

There came a stage when municipal councillors of Bombay stated the bottom line, in the media.

"If no rain falls within the week, we run out of drinking water and Mumbai will have to be evacuated."

Exactly what 'evacuated' meant was anybody's guess. Like Fatehpur-Sikri during Mughal-times? Evacuate and go where? Evacuate five million citizens. How?

In Dev Anand's milestone film *Guide* (1965) – coincidentally produced during the drought period – singer, maestro and music-composer Sachin Dev Burman himself sings to his own tunes:

"Allah mere, pani deh … Rama mere, pani deh"

"Oh God! Please create the conditions for precipitation to occur… please give us rain…"

Suddenly everybody became religious. Hindus and Muslims were singing S.D. Burman's song, either loudly in the streets or softly in their hearts.

I had a gut-feeling that something would definitely, finally happen.

There would be a sudden loud rumbling, followed by a gigantic cloudburst. Heavy drops of the precious hydrogen and oxygen combination would make their way to earth. I had seen this happen somewhere before. There would be a mysterious background musical score accompanying the thunderclap and suddenly sexy Marathi women clad in dark red and green saris would appear, wearing custom-designed buns on their heads and waterproof orange-coloured lipstick, their cheeks glowing with genuine Eastman Colour rouge. They would all dance to the clamorous tunes of Bappi Lahiri, along with scrawny men who looked like they were just fished out of a trawler in the Arabian Sea, paid fifty rupees and a scarf each, and told to dance.

Every soul in Bombay would get into the act. Rich and poor. Males, females and others. Workers and the unemployed. Taxis and buses would wade through two-metre deep puddles without switching off; splashing tidal waves of water onto smiling pedestrians, who would not mind in the least, but would also join the continuous score.

Passing scholars would abandon school and turn their umbrellas upside down and watch them float

Letter to Hawabai (c. September 1967)

away on the rivers and streams that were once foot-paths and motorways.

What bullshit.

When the drought ended and the skies opened, the sudden monsoon brought with it a disaster of its own. Floods, damaged homes, collapsed buildings, destroyed informal settlements, mudslides, broken electrical communications, stranded passengers, can-celled flights, drownings, vehicles swept off bridges, bridges washed away and children missing. All with-out a background musical score.

SAGAAI

In South Africa, Father was a real economiser. He was a miser. My allowance for years, even during high school, seldom exceeded ten cents a day and fif-ty cents for the weekend. This was supposed to cover a trip to the cinema as well.

I was, therefore, blown out of my mind when he ac-tually purchased a three-bedroom flat for my exclu-sive use, while I was a student at Andheri.

I enquired about his generosity.

"You have been through a hectic time so far in India, Eb. Surviving vomit-inducing jaundice, becom-ing traumatised by the war between India and Paki-stan, gritting your teeth and touring Fatehpur-Sikri with your aunt, battling with your exams, coming to terms with recent droughts, and, of course, being booted out of Bengal."

I argued that I had not been kicked out by the Howrah College. I had withdrawn because they did not offer me the course I had been selected for. He disagreed and told me to shut up.

My own flat in a foreign country. This was bewildering.

What would my friends at the hostel say? I began to project comments:

Friend (1): "You lucky dog!"

Friend (2): "Your dad's a God!"

Friend (3): "Impossible."

Friend (4): "Not feasible."

Friend (5): "Unreasonable."

Friend (6): "Can I move in with you?"

Friend (100): "Can I move in with you?"

Friend (401): "Can I…?"

Those last echoing comments were enough. It would put paid to my privacy and also destroy Father's expensive objective of giving me an opportunity to be independent of external and unnecessary stresses. The aim was to taste another side of the country. The problem was that it would be awkward to refuse my best friends.

There had to be a solution to ward off my friends, the parasites. I came up with a devious solution.

I requested Father to order a nameplate for the front door and would pretend I was a paying guest of the person whose name was on that nameplate. So if anyone had to ask if I stayed alone in the fully furnished flat, I would have an answer.

And if there was a follow-up question of "But where are the owners?", I could reply:

"Well, they are business people from Gujarat, who come by every so often. They might even come tonight. Darn it. Always cramping my style."

I hated lying. But my friends hated honesty. So what could I do?

Rajinder Krishan's lyrics in *Sagaai* (1949) summed it up.

"Jukthi hain duniya … Jukhaneh wala chahiyeh"

"A sucker is born every minute"

The nameplate read: Mr EB KOYBIE.

In Memon, this roughly translates to *'And for that matter, anybody'*. The ambiguity became a running gag for me and Father and annoyed the hell out of my friends.

NAAG DEVTA

Our flat in Andheri was in a building called Ratan-Deep. Father had gone to great lengths to provide me a comfortable environment so I could study in peace. It was fully furnished and even had two balconies that faced Swami Vivekanand Road. He had even arranged an old woman to cook for me. Her husband worked as a builder, handyman and a security guard for the developer of the building, a Mr. Sadruddin Nanavati.

I was blessed with neighbours, on either side of my second floor flat. Both belonged to the Jain faith. This religious group is so committed to nonviolence that very staunch Jain monks would wear face masks to prevent hurting airborne germs. Some would steer clear of certain fruits that have gone past midseason to ensure they did not kill the eggs of worms – un-hatched and invisible – but alive within the fruit.

In other words, they worship all forms of life. One thing was for certain, both my Jain friends, Shantilal and Dhananjay, worshipped the ground on which I walked. And the feeling was mutual. We doused each other with equal amounts of harmless coloured water during the colourful Indian festival of Holi.

There were other Jains living on the ground floor.

I recall an incident, when I was returning from college and was confronted with a big, brown snake in the middle of my path. Instinctively, I grabbed a brick and was about to crush the reptile's head when the head of the nearest household, a Mr Swami, came rushing out screaming, "No, Mr Essa! Not like that!"

"We cannot kill the snake until we know that it is genuinely harmful," he added calmly.

I smiled. And walked briskly away. I was not about to find out if the snake was harmful. "Perhaps, next time, Mr Swami," I thought to myself, "I will take a taxi to the Bombay Zoological Museum, check out the reptile catalogue, match the snake and return to kill or kiss its arse!"

GUIDE

Indian actor Dev Anand was always my favourite. Was it because he often bagged the best melodies set to unusual tunes by the Bengali master of music, S.D Burman? Or was it because he often played the un-derdog, as in *Baazi* (1951) *Pocket Maar* (1956) and *Taxi Driver* (1954)? Or because he always acted opposite pretty and very talented actresses like petite Wahee-da Rehman, sophisticated Nutan, or spontaneous Geeta Bali?

I think the main reason that I loved him was that he acted as if he could not act.

His pants were often baggy, a bit too broad or a bit too short, but Dev enjoyed the reputation of being the fastest talker on the Indian screen. Whereas Dilip

My sister Halima was always such a poser (c. 1967)

My cousin Baboo (centre) at his wedding around 1967. I am in the bow tie to his left.

Kumar would choose to deliver dialogue in a slow, deliberate, ball-by-ball style, Dev could rattle the entire Bhagavad Gita from end to end in one breath

I really wanted to meet him. So imagine my dismay, anger and envy when I learned one day that a group of South African students – some of them my best friends and ex-roommates from the National Union – announce that they have just returned from visiting the star himself at his Juhu residence.

When I question them as to why they hadn't invited me to come with them, they burst into laughter.

Kadwa: "Go kiss Koybie's arse" - in reference to my fictitious landlord at Ratan Deep.

Saloojee: "You are living in the lap of luxury so why bother yourself with leaving your ivory tower *just* to visit stupid Indian movie stars?"

Their comments hurt me. I couldn't believe they had called Dev stupid.

Kotwal then went to some lengths to describe their interview with the star, "Essa, you should have listened to his accent and how he pronounced English words. In fact, Jyoti actually laughed out loud."

Apparently Dev was polite, but he didn't like that they poked fun at him.

When I returned to the flat, I thought about what I had heard. I became overwhelmed with rage.

Here was an opportunity for young South African students to link up with a famous and celebrated film star. They could have discussed culture and cinema and exchanged ideas. Instead, these arrogant idiots from Dhakshan Africa chose to focus on the great star's accent!?

Did they actually believe that their South African accent – picked up from rubbing noses with other

South Africans for the last hundred years – actually made them smarter or more advanced?

This perceived superiority complex reminded me of what I had noticed during my voyage on the S.S. Kampala six months prior. South African Indians demonstrated more violent tendencies compared to the East African Indians who had come aboard from Mombasa. There were all sorts of physical punch-ups on board and most of it was one sided. The South Africans beating the hell out of other Indians for the most trivial reasons.

I wondered what exactly had made us this way?

Was it the repression of Apartheid?

The average Indian, in Durban especially, always felt sandwiched between being intimidated by Black Africans and bullied by whites. Especially since January 1949, when the notorious race riots in Mayville had taken place. And especially since 1950, when the Group Areas Act had been imposed.

Even at Bhavan's College, local students that I freely socialised with complained that they were secretly afraid of the average South African Indian student.

Back home, whites called us by the derogatory term: 'coolies'. Here in India, South Africans of Indian origin, chose to address local Indians as 'char-ous' in a condescending, offensive manner.

Could the issue be a matter of self-hatred?

AGNI PAREEKSHA
Before Father returned to South Africa, he advised me to do something about my weakest subject, Mathematics, by recruiting a private tutor. I was finally able to convince a college professor to assist me, for

Pilot of the mad age – me in Pahalgam, Kashmir (c. 1967)

a nominal fee and had lessons twice a week at his semi-detached townhouse close to the railway crossing, in Saki Naka, a neighbourhood in Andheri-East.

After many weeks of regular tuition, I felt confident about the upcoming midterms.

I was due to write Calculus as a full-scale examination. After failing every class test dismally, I had to pass this examination or be forced to repeat the year.

On the eve of the exam, I began to feel the ghosts of past failure visiting me. Burning the oil far past midnight, I revised each and every type of problem that could possibly appear. In fact, I studied till 5am, slept for about two hours, enjoyed a cold shower, and a hot breakfast prepared by the Shantabai, the maid. I finally made my way to college, excited about the paper. This was probably the first time I had ever looked forward to a math exam.

When the paper was passed out, I perused the pages and revelled; the questions looked familiar. All that extra tuition had paid off, and last night's extra work had been well worth losing sleep over.

Just after the first question, however, there seemed to be something strange about the other candidates, the furniture, the ceiling – everything seemed to be spinning. I was overcome with nausea.

"Oh NO! God! Please! Not now! Not when I know most of the answers. Please let me be able to see this through.

The invigilator, a young lecturer studying for his master's degree in science, noticed that I was not looking well. He came up to me and asked whether I wished to continue with the exam. He could see that I was in no condition to do so but whispered, most tactfully and politely, that once exams began I could not change my mind.

*From left: Granny,
Hawabai, Fathima,
Mother, Halima, Father,
Walla and Ahmed at
Durban Airport.
Mother and Halima were
enroute to visit me in
Bombay (c. 1967)*

I was devastated. The initial light-headed feeling had given way to a heavy migraine. I put my head down on the desk, closed my eyes and tried to doze off for a few minutes in the hope that the pain would pass. It did not. Intermittently, I picked up my pen and attempted some answers, placing my head down again after a few minutes. When I walked out of that examination room, I was in tears but too sick to sob.

I returned to Ratan Deep on that sad Saturday afternoon, and without my customary shower, or a meal, or changing into my pajamas, I swallowed two tablets for nausea, switched off all the lights and fell into bed. As my nausea began to wear off, I began to think straight again. I saw the reality. I had certainly failed calculus again. Why?

I felt absolutely destroyed. All that sacrifice. All that effort! What more did I need to do? What answers would I give to Father? I found myself sobbing, all alone in the darkness of my flat in Andheri.

I was due to write physics the next morning. Another killer. Forget it. Don't write it. Fail it too. I resolve to go back home a laughing stock.

The next morning I wake to ferocious knocking at the door. It is Shantabai. She must have been banging at the door since 6 am., if not the entire night. She is screaming in Marathi. I unlatch the door and go back to sleep. But she comes to the bedroom and continues screaming.

"What is wrong with you? You did not answer the door since last night. Have you eaten? I thought you were studying? You writing an exam today. In one hour. No?!"

*Top: Shantabai's
son, Manoj (left)
(c. 1968)*

*Right: Shantabai
with her daughter
(c. 1968)*

"It is no use Shantabai. I messed up yesterday's paper. I am going to fail. It is over," I reply.

I felt her very thin hands grabbing me and dragging me out of bed.

"Is this why your father got you this flat? Stop feeling sorry for yourself. You go wash your face. I will make tea and you have to go. Fast. Fast."

Here was Shantabai, illiterate and living in abject poverty, with Shankar bhai, a drunkard for a husband and a 10-year-old son named Manoj who had already been pulled out of school to help earn a living for the family, trying desperately to motivate an irrelevant foreigner to stop moping around and do the right thing.

I felt even more sick.

But I got off the bed. I wrote the physics exam and passed. By some miracle from heaven I managed to scrape a pass in Calculus, too.

Postscript

In 1969, I returned to South Africa.

When I had first made the journey, the SS Kampala had taken 21 days to reach India. The new French liners took 12 days. Later, Italian liners would take no more than eight days.

I remember feeling confused about my return home.

I had come to "do Engineering" but had left with a costly and ambiguous BSc degree, which promised little in terms of a career.

India had become my home as well. Where and to what was I returning, I could not fathom.

But before we left, we had some work to do.

The flat at Andheri had to be emptied. I had no idea where to begin. The flat keys were to be handed to 'a contact' who would sell the flat for us. We got Rs.38000 for it in 1970. I am really uncertain about how we finally packed everything in one taxi and boarded that French boat at Ballard Pier.

Since we couldn't eat the meat on the ship, given our halaal ways, we were restricted to bland vegetables and some dodgy soup broth.

Mealtimes used to be announced over the ship intercom. "Lunch for the 3rd class passengers is being served".

For which I had my own modification "Lunch for the pigs on the lower gallery is now being served" – which is exactly how it felt.

I also decided to keep in touch with Shantabai and used to send her money from time to time. After some time, her husband died from cirrhosis of the liver. Then her only potential hope for survival, Manoj, was fatally run over by a bus. I have no idea what became of her second child, her daughter. Finally, I lost all trace of Shantabai, too.

My BSc was not very useful. And to avoid being put behind a shop counter, I tried to make in-roads in electrical engineering. But it didn't go far. I managed to get an apprenticeship in 1971 in Verulam. I took the train at 6am and returned at 6pm for R100 a month. Besides breaking my finger in the factory, narrowly avoiding electrocution from high-tension wires and contracting bronchitis, the apprenticeship went by without too many hazards. Even though I was working with and for white South Africans, the amenities were all separate; be it the train ride or the toilets. They were also obsessed with curry.

The Story of my Father
SULIMAN ESSA PATEL (1910-1974)

My Father had a special clause in his will that asked for his life story to be made available to his family and associates upon his passing.

It read: "So my family will know that when your intentions are good, and when you are prepared to work and sweat to achieve your goals, nothing in life becomes impossible – this inspiration I give to you with Faith, Love and Pride".

In 1979, five years after his death, I put together a short biography, reproduced here.

Mud & Poverty

8000km north-east of Durban, across the vast Indian Ocean; 500km north of Bombay, lies a small village of mud huts, surrounded by the ruins of the wall of a one-time fort, which silently speaks of a past, unknown glory.

The inhabitants are mostly farmers, traders or labourers. Many of them have no means of livelihood.

Hindu and Moslem men, hardly distinguishable from each other, go about their lazy business, with turbans to protect them from the noonday heat. Women are rarely seen. Those that are, gather at waterholes, and near the river. Hindu women wear bright and colourful saris, whilst their Moslem counterparts hide their features behind black burkas.

The common language is "Kutchi" or "Memon", a dialect concocted from Gujarati and Sindhi; the latter hinting at the far-northern origin of these people.

There are few shops. Naked children scamper through the dirty, muddy streets. Oxcarts work their way quietly, from one end of the village to the other. The atmosphere is one of quiet desolation and shameless poverty.

This is Jodiya, 1910.

Birth of a Star
Amid the dung, dirt, poverty and illiteracy; was born in an average home, to average parents, a child who would prove not to be of that world, years ahead of his time, and most certainly the very basis for the existence of our family in South Africa.

My father, Suliman Essa Patel, born in Jodiya on 25 December, 1910 .

The population could not have exceeded 6000 then. Livelihood in the village depended on minor agricultural activities with smaller villages, lying towards the east.

Father wrote:

"I remember my younger days, from the time I was hardly four. We were living in a family house – partly double-storey in front, and rather well ventilated, except for the room where I was born. I cannot recall any sanitation or adequate fresh water. The only ventilation was through gaps in the mud tiles placed on a split bamboo frame. Dust used to filter through these gaps on windy days, keeping the room always dirty."

Food & Fuel

"I remember breakfast consisted of stale, toasted thick roti, made of gram flour, left over from the previous night's meal. Nothing more. Lunch was made up of fresh roti (bajra or jawar), sometimes with vegetable curry, always with chhas (sour milk, diluted in water). Porridge with milk, or chhas was the usual supper. Ghee, although about 10c/kg, was a luxury my family could not afford."

What Father writes about his mother, is a rather interesting account of the hard life of even the average woman in those days.

"I remember my mother getting up at 2am and going to the far away fields with other women, to collect wood, to be used as fuel in the rainy season. She often used to return after noon! My grandmother, who was the grand old lady of the house, used to look after me, my younger brother Dawood, and sister Amina."

Childhood Conditions

Living conditions in those days reeked of grim desolation. Death by disease or even drowning was common. Epidemics came in regular cycles. Deadly eye diseases such as trachoma during hot and dusty months (May and June), were followed by malaria, cholera and influenza during the monsoon. Winter brought smallpox, measles and chickenpox. Infant mortality was high. One of every two babies died within a year. Half of those surviving did not reach the age of three and those that did had to contend with the diseases mentioned above! "I am unable to explain how I survived," my Father said.

He continues, "The only set of clothes I owned was the one I had on. When it came to washing this set, I had to play in the river whilst my mother washed and dried my clothes."

Father paints a picture of himself as a ragamuffin, running about barefoot, contracting at different times of his childhood, measles, malaria, chickenpox and other terrible diseases. And this was merely the picture of a better-than-average child in any village in India, at the time!

Early Education
He was under five when he was admitted to Gujarati school; successfully passing every year right up to Standard 3. He was probably the brightest student in his class, without receiving any guidance at home. He had an excellent memory and also excelled in sports.

Unfortunately a change occurred on being promoted to Standard 4. He had to attend school a long distance from home. His father, meanwhile, was charged with arson, in South Africa. This caused Father endless worry. During the same period, his two uncles Abasoomar and Joosabally, arrived from South Africa.

Seeing them for the first time caused a minor sensation. All the above conspired to cause him to lose interest in his studies. He lost a few weeks at school, resulting in a gap in learning – especially in mathematics – which he could not reconcile. He then began to revolt and play truant. After failing Standard 4, he left school, and continued at madrassah for a short while, until his father's return from South Africa.

My father talks of his father's trading days, in India.

"My father went to Barar – quite a distance away in the early days – to earn a living. He was often away for eight months, in a year. I joined him after I left school; hawking bangles, textiles and other fancy goods, travelling from village to village in a hired bullock cart."

At other times my Father sold glass bangles and sweets, walking alone in the hot sun, barefoot.

Departure for Africa

Leaving Jodiya in 1925, when he was only about 15, Father describes the strange sensation of seeing the "outside" world for the first time.

"In Bombay, meals cost about a cent in restaurants. It was all very thrilling until I got on board the boat, with about 2000 passengers, living like animals. I felt sad, often weeping with homesickness. I thought of my mother, brothers, sisters and friends, constantly. Would I ever meet them again? As the ship moved further and further away all day, all hopes for the things behind me faded. This hopelessness was replaced by an even worse apprehension of the things that lay ahead of me, of which I had no idea, whatsoever!"

In South Africa for the first time

Suliman arrived on 25 March 1925 and put up with Osman Dada near the mosque, for a few days. He then proceeded to Pietermaritzburg. Having found no opening there, he tried Vryheid and other places in the Transvaal, but with no real luck. He did odd jobs, often just for meals and a place to sleep in return.

He finally returned to Durban, in 1928 and worked at the Point (Dock area) for about R3.00 per month. The job entailed getting up at 5am and going to bed at 10pm daily.

He returned to India with his grandfather in 1928, to get married. His grandfather did not return to South Africa after that trip.

Father remained in India till April 1930 and then returned to South Africa. He worked at Retief Street. in Pietermaritzburg for about R4.00 per month. This period coincided with the Great Depression sweeping the entire world, causing extreme hardship to many. He cannot recall why he left his job but does recall, buying a sewing machine and doing patch work for a living. He managed to accumulate about R400 and left again for India in 1934, remaining there for about two and a half years.

Bringing the family home

Father recalls the circumstances under which he managed to bring the rest of the family to South Africa.

"My grandfather and grandmother were nearly 80, an age when they certainly needed somebody to look after their welfare. Yet they – my grandmother in particular – insisted I take the family and "get out of this hellhole" as soon as possible. She went to the extent of selling her jewellery and other precious possessions to pay for the fares."

Years later, in 1970, on visiting the graves of these two brave people, he asked himself, "What was the mission of these, my grandparents, lying there and left behind to fend for themselves? Surely the answer was a sacrifice for the betterment of the younger family! Ahmed, Mariambai, Ismail and Mahomed must remember that had it not been for this great sacrifice no one can ascertain what course events would have taken, or how their lives would have turned out!"

My Father himself took a big chance in bringing the rest of his family to South Africa, without consulting his father, who had no intention of doing so at that stage.

He had to return to South Africa within a certain period (or lose his right to do so, forever!) but became involved in the marriage cancellation of a near relative, which sparked some hostility and grew to become a drawn-out legal issue. This drove him to change his return period through extreme transport problems and severe red tape, making it to South Africa with the family, in August 1937, just ten days before the deadline.

In Durban they lived in a hired flat (up to recently Lodson House, now above Hansa's Cafe, Prince Edward Street). Part of Father's immediate family had been left behind – his daughter, Hawabai and her mother – whose papers had still not come through. They arrived in Durban ten months later. Father comments that it took Hawabai – who had been only 15 months old when he left India – more than a month to take to him again!

Making a Living
Father described how he joined his father in the demolition business. Household expenses were about R30.00 per month plus rent. During the weekends and between demolition jobs, he would help out at 48 Harbottle Road, Overport. This continued till early 1939. The business included selling timber. During

the Second World War – which lasted until 1945 – him and his family joined a sawmill and box factory at Main Road in Mayville, Durban.

In 1949, Suliman joined Baker Bros as a partner.

"I drew about R12.00 per week from this business. This was insufficient to pay for household expenses, and usually the rent was not paid for the house at 48 Windsor Road, Mayville, owned by my father."

The last of this rent was finally paid in installments, on the 5 April 1963, a mere ten years before he passed away. This came as quite a shock to his immediate family, who thought they were always well off.

Father, on R12.00 per week, was once faced with a grim situation, where I was suffering from a severe asthma attack. As the evening drew nearer, the attack became heavier.

"At about 9pm, I told myself that I could not afford a doctor – but how could I allow the child to suffer through the night? I finally called Dr Naidoo, who came about 10pm. His account was about £5.00 (a small fortune in those days!), which had to be booked down. This was the heavy price which had to be paid for a child's sound sleep."

Listening to this account, touched me deeply.

He left Baker Bros and joined Andy's Scrap Yard as a partner in 1950. This was a profitable business except for a lot of waste and theft, which forced him to finally leave in August 1954. He sold his share to Andrew for R12000.00. This is the equivalent of at least R50,000.00 today.) His drawings had been about R100.00 per month at first, but grew to R150.00. After Andy's he went back to India to settle some legal issues, and returned almost penniless in 1956.

He then began Sepson Trading Company at 91 Albert Street in 1957; delivering goods himself by van, to the Transvaal, and other areas. He then entered into partnership with an old friend, Jamnadas. He recalls bitterly that the partnership did not turn out for the good, and was dissolved within a year. A new chapter opened for Father.

The Tide Turns
Father opened Bombay House on his own strength, in November, 1959. This ladies fancy goods and imitation jewellery business was a turning point in Father's long, hard struggle. He emphasises the vital role his son Mohammed Yusuf – who intended to pursue a B.Com university degree, but joined the business instead – played in making a success of Bombay House.

"We started Bombay House from scratch. And after much hard work, frequently working past midnight, and on weekends, all the time enjoying the cooperation of a deeply united and honest family, we emerged as giants. Without Mohammed Yusuf, Halima, and later, Fathima, this business could not have been what it is today!"

Today, his children are financially independent only because Bombay House could afford them first-class careers.

In Retrospect
The above is the story derived from Father's own writings.

And these are my observations:

He never knew the meaning of defeat or fear, and set himself far horizons with his daring attitude, positive foresight and neverending enthusiasm. Even when a major financial catastrophe hit him in the forties, and he lost all his hard-earned savings, leaving him completely penniless, he himself paid the heaviest price and bore the blame on himself. He never allowed this terrible tragedy to cast shadows on his children or family, but with deep-rooted grit and confidence he rebuilt his life from scratch.

He repaid all the family and friends who assisted him during this tragedy as soon as the funds came into his hands and had earned enough to maintain a simple standard of living for his family. The luxury of a car or new furniture or other "unnecessary" spending was never mentioned or desired, not until his moral obligation of paying off his debts was fulfilled.

This "starting from scratch and making it to the top once more" gave him the greatest satisfactiona and pleasure in his whole life, and made him a much more "lovable" and "gay" person.

He was never spineless or found lacking in enterprise. Adventure was in his blood from an early age. From exploring the country, to hunting, to taking up a challenge; right up to producing an Indian film in India in 1955, that was my Father.

Honesty, giving of himself, keeping his promises, empathising with the ill, playing with children, accepting all kinds of change, sincerity, appreciating and acknowledging every small favour, paying all his debts, playing an able nurse to the sick at home, and giving frank advice on domestic matters, earned him the respect of friend and foe; even those who did not like his attitude or frankness.

Apart from a few minor weaknesses – a nasty temper in particular – Father was an uncanny personality and a giant of a man, in every respect. He was a chronic asthmatic but by sheer diet control made this seem non-existent. He always looked far younger than his years and was dead set against excess of any nature; smoking, gambling and drinking.

I recall an incident when I asked Father if I could try some champagne left over from a party which he had given to certain participants in the putting up of the building at Teakwood Road. I said, "Dad, I am also against liquor but just to see how it tastes, for fun?!" He gave me a stern look and replied, "And suppose you like the taste?!" The author has never forgotten this bit of philosophy.

Modesty was always his strong point. He never made a show of being charitable, although he supported a number of people, and contributed regularly to registered charities. He was against commonplace begging.

Despite his minimal education he had a head for figures. I often tried competing with him, using "superior" log tables and slide-rules, but always lost to Suliman's super built-in computer.

The vast amount of general knowledge stored in that head would have put any encyclopaedia to shame! He fully understood the politics of nearly all major countries. When it came to India, besides being extremely proud of his Indian heritage – he actually teared when Jawarlal Nehru's death was announced over the radio – he had a thorough understanding of her ancient history and modern policies. His comprehension of all facets of civil and commercial law was fascinating, and many friends had sought legal advice from him.

He never once turned anybody away, no matter how busy he might have been. His brand of humour was quaint. He was always prepared to appreciate a joke, a quality rather uncommon among his generation. His religious ideas were always based on logic, sound reasoning and facts; instead of the usual emotion, fear, tradition or sentiment. He was a firm believer that any good should be done for its own sake and not merely to obtain credit for the hereafter. I doubt if he believed in any hereafter at all!

Traditional customs meant nothing to him, if they were not based on common sense. He hated narrow-mindedness and communal fanaticism, never criticising any religion or undermining any race.

His hatred for superstition was extraordinary. Especially when it came to indoctrinating young children with ideas carried over for generations, but which had no logical basis, and which did more harm than good. He was prepared to oppose those ideas tooth and nail.

It was rather ironic, then, that he included the following little episode on how he obtained the name "Suliman". But this is in keeping with his tongue-in-cheek humour.

"My fui, Fatima had taken a vow that on the birth of the first male child to my father, the child was to be named at the tomb of Datar Peer near Junagadh, Saurastra, India. Being ignorant of this vow, my parents named me Abdulkarim. On being enlightened of the vow, this name was withdrawn and I suddenly became nameless. The name 'giga', meaning male baby, being used in the interim, until I was three!

I was then taken to the durga, situated on the peak of a mountain called Gir (a nature reserve, where even tigers are found). It is reached it after a three-hour plus climb over steps round the mountain. The steps were about 2 ½ metres wide and 20cm high, with landings for resting at various points. Many people were going up and down – and others taking a rest on the way. The Durga itself is in a cave.

The mujawar made me sit in front of him, gave me a pedda and a half-shell (coconut) of holy water (which drips overhead, in the cave, day and night). He then called out "Suliman" and the name stuck!"

I must make special mention of the amount of re-spect people had for him.

This is certainly not surprising to those who knew him as a person who was always ready to help some-body in need. Perhaps he never forgot his own pover-ty-stricken background.

I always found him down-to-earth, never snobbish and never prepared to accept any norms at their tradi-tional face value. He often questioned unnecessary red tape but never forced other people to accept his way. His arguments were always based on logic.

I also want to add a point about hygiene. He was always neat, he often washed his own clothes. Food and utensils had to be extremely clean, or he would blow his top! Ironically, Father was to lose his life through a possible slip up on the part of a hotel kitch-en's hygiene, which caused him food poisoning.

In Conclusion

To me, he was a loving father who made certain his children were never in want of anything (a privilege he never enjoyed in his own childhood). But he was careful not to spoil his children. Everybody had to dig-in when it came to running the business. Al-though never a miser, he was against needless waste and extravagance.

He really loved being with his family and would never shy away from joining them in games or picnics.

The building that he engineered – at Teakwood Road, Jacobs – was his very own brainchild, and the sweat he put into this project right from start to finish is something which cannot be easily forgotten.

And all for what?

So that his children would enjoy a bright, secure future, surely?

Alas, just when everything was working according to plan and he was about to retire, and watch his family enjoy the fruit of all the hard labour he had put into his own life over forty years in South Africa, Death snatched him on the 15th April 1974, dealing an unexpectedly cruel blow to all of us.

IN MEMORIAM

The death of Grandfather Essa, in 1973 had a profound effect on my Father.

Recollections of his childhood days; his pleasant memories with his father, their toil and struggle together to set the family up; and the adventures and experiences they alone had shared together in India and South Africa, reeled through his mind, and it took more than six months to get over the emptiness and loneliness. He had truly lost more than a Father and a friend!

But death is always cruel. Death is nearly always unexpected, too. But in this case, I wonder if he had any regrets.

Could any man have lived a more amazing or full life?

Ebrahim Essa
Durban (1979)

Acknowledgments

It takes a village to pull a book together.

I want to start by acknowledging Dr. Rob Pattman and Dr. Sultan Khan, who in 2007, included Dad's article on cinema in Grey Street in the remarkable anthology "Undressing Durban". The inclusion of his article provided impetus for a larger project like this one today.

Still, convincing Dad to write down his stories was difficult initially. But once he started, it was clear that nothing besides a cursory cautioning about the paper supply was going to stop him.

Hundreds of pages were scribbled and later typed up by two colleagues at Crescent Girls High where he taught Physical Science.

To Farzana Shaikh and Mariam Yedhub, thank you for making sense of the scribbles and for encouraging Dad that this project was worth it.

Soon enough, photos needed to be scanned and chapters needed to be sent to me via email.

Enter Muhammed and Raheema Mitha who sat patiently with Dad, helped digitize photos, and sent updated chapters to me, whether I was in Doha or elsewhere. I appreciate your efforts, too.

The book also benefited from the goodwill of many others:

Mishka Wazar for the first round of copy edits, endless questions, and for typing up the final chapter.

Samina Anwary who stepped in like a breath of fresh air. Samina treated the stories as if they belonged to her own family. She gave the book a careful second copy-edit, typeset it and designed the epic cover.

It would be remiss of me not to thank my Uncle Walla (whom I call Big Daddy), Uncle Ahmed, Uncle Mini-Ebrahim, Hawa-fui, Halima fui and my cousin Ikbal Moosa for being such a spirited part of this adventure, too.

And finally, I want to thank my mother, Rooksana, who has always been the first port of call for all our stories.

It was just over five years ago that I received an email with the complete manuscript from Dad that read: "That's it! Now the ball is in your court."

It took me five years to put it all together; to delete, organise and curate. I guess without my Hafsa reminding me on the daily to make sure I get it done, it might have taken me five more years.

I feel immensely privileged to have been given the responsibility to take care of this work of history. I know my sister Shenaaz is proud of the work Dad has put into this.

I just hope it resonates.

Azad Essa
October 2019